WHEN THE RED LIGHT GOES ON, GET OFF
A LIFE IN COMEDY

This is for my father, John Malcolm Wing,
a lifelong student of comedy who loves to laugh.

And for my mother, Angela Adele Wing,
who bought me Richard Pryor's 'Bicentennial Nigger' album
for my seventeenth birthday.

Thank you. Thank you very much.

The Black Moss Press Settlements series gives writers a creative non-fiction forum for focusing on their roots, the "place" out of which their writing has emerged, and the study of the craft itself.

Books in the Settlements series include:

The Farm On The Hill He Calls Home, by John B. Lee – #1
Calling The Wild, by Roger Hilles – #2
Riding On A Magpie Riff, by Richard Stevenson – #3
When The Earth Was Flat, Raymond Fraser – #4
Left Hand Horses, John B. Lee – #5
The Gargoyle's Left Ear, by Susan McMaster – #6
When the Red Light Goes On, Get Off, by John Wing – #7

When the Red Light Goes On, Get Off

A Life in Comedy
by John Wing, Jr.

EARLY DAYS ON STAGE: Of course, the idea of being a stand-up comedian simply wasn't practical. This was Canada.

Black Moss Press
2008

Library and Archives Canada Cataloguing in Publication

Wing, John, 1959-.

When the red light goes on, get off : a life in comedy / John Wing, Jr.

ISBN 978-0-88753-455-3

1. Wing, John, 1959-. 2. Comedians--Canada--Biography. 3. Poets, Canadian (English)--20th century--Biography. I. Title.

PS8595.I5953Z477 2008   792.702'8092   C2008-903596-8

Published by Black Moss Press, 2450 Byng Road, Windsor, Ontario N8W 3E8. Black Moss Press books are distributed by LitDistco, and all orders should be directed there.

Black Moss acknowledges the generous support for its publishing program from The Canada Council for the Arts and The Ontario Arts Council.

ONTARIO ARTS COUNCIL
CONSEIL DES ARTS DE L'ONTARIO

Le Conseil des Arts | The Canada Council
du Canada | for the Arts

CONTENTS

THE RED LIGHT BANDIT

THE VERY FIRST joke I recall is from Felix The Cat. I was probably six or seven and had finally graduated from Beany and Cecil and moved on at last to more sophisticated television fare. Felix was attempting to set up a deck chair for sunbathing, and the chair was being, in a word, recalcitrant. Each time he would lie down it would throw a fit and imprison him after a series of gyrations. Finally, exasperated as only a cartoon cat can be, he said, "That chair is a menace. I wouldn't touch it with a ten foot pole. Luckily, I have an eleven foot pole." You could even make a case that it was the first dick joke I ever heard, although that is stretching it a bit. It would have to be from a Weekly World News headline. CAT BORN WITH ELEVEN FOOT SCHLONG! SEE THE FORMIDABLE FERAL FELINE PENIS!

You get the point. Remembering jokes is something standup comedians do very well. I might not know a joke when you first ask me – "Did you hear the one about the cat with the really long–?" but I'll have figured it out before you're even halfway through telling it, first because I know formulas and how a joke works, and second because it takes you so long to tell the bloody thing. Brevity, people, brevity.

When I was a boy, I watched an amazing amount of comedy on

television. Jack Benny, George Burns, Jackie Gleason and Art Carney, Red Skelton, and the Ed Sullivan comics. I remember watching Bert Lahr do a 'Doctor as Blind Butcher' sketch on Sullivan when I was perhaps seven years old. He was so nearsighted that he thought a skeleton was a real person. When his living patient ran off in comic horror, Bert closed the sketch by turning to the skeleton and saying, "You are next, Mr. Davis." Why I remember such things is a mystery to me. In the late sixties, I recall watching Alan King a great deal. He was a master of the slow burn and the rhythmic word announcing a new level of anger. His comedy was not physical at all, other than facial expressions and posture changes, which were very subtle compared to Red Skelton or Gleason or Carney. Flip Wilson was a favourite of my father, and on his show (sponsored in Canada by Genuine Kraft slices) I first saw Franklin Ajaye, Willie Tyler and Lester, and the young George Carlin, just entering his first hippie phase. We began to accumulate comedy albums in our house, starting with Alan Sherman's 'My Son, The Celebrity', followed by David Frye's 'I Am The President (And Make No Mistake About That)', and finally, George Carlin's first three, 'AM/FM', 'Class Clown' and 'Occupation: Foole'. I wore out those records, and can still quote great chunks of them today.

Then, in 1970, we somehow came into possession of the classic, 'Monty Python's Previous Record'. An astounding piece of work. Eric the Half a Bee, The Argument Clinic, and a piece done by Eric Idle that made me laugh harder than I ever had before, and possibly since. It was a monologue called 'A Minute Passed'. I will attempt it from memory. "Slowly, hesitantly, Helen slipped out of a thin, tight-waisted bodysuit and stood naked before me in the moonlight. Somewhere a clock chimed three. An owl hooted in the nearby copse. No wind stirred the casement window as she stood in the pale translucent light before me. A minute passed. And then another. Then another minute passed. I waited a moment, while a minute passed quickly past. Then a minute which seemed to last an hour but was only a minute, passed. (Announcer): That was 'A Minute Passed' by Roger Finlayson. You can hear it again tomorrow night, at a minute past." That's not verbatim, of course. It seems shorter and I'm sure I'm missing some of it. But I could not stop laughing when I first heard it. By the time I was thirteen years old in 1972 and began watching Johnny Carson regularly, I had a giant file of jokes and sketches in my head. To this day, lines will jump out suddenly, like pop-up windows, and confuse the hell out of whomever I'm with, unless it's my brother Richard, who has the same backlog of recalled material. When we get together, it can be an endless shorthand of our favourite lines. Richard became a teacher, and uses his memory flash drive to excellent effect with his students. I went another way.

I have been a professional standup comedian now for 28 years, and most people have rather lofty ideas about my business. They think it's a very glamorous life; the travel, the bright lights, the meeting famous people, et cetera. And those aspects are certainly pleasant. But of course that's only a small portion of my life. The majority of it is long lines in airports, long flights, long drives, small rooms, and being alone. I'm very good at being alone. It's a requirement. The other requirements are a deep, indexed, and easily accessible memory. (No Fact Too Trivial! No Word Too Small!) That memory must include your own life experience as well, and you can't ever be worried about how a family member will react to your portrayal of him or her. Self absorption always helps, although your act and career are the only place it's helpful. Everywhere else it's a problem. A decent work ethic, especially in the beginning, is necessary. An analytical mind, a love of pop culture and weird ideas, and a smart mouth are all good things for the resume. Let's see, what else? Oh, right. Some talent. That certainly helps. Stage presence, too. And, of course, an inexhaustible tolerance for bullshit, which is what you must wade through to get onstage. Always. Still.

There have been glamorous nights, of course. I have opened for The Smothers Brothers, Robert Hunter of The Grateful Dead, John Raitt, The Mills Brothers, Gloria DeHaven, and Tony Martin, to name a few. Before the show, Tony Martin introduced me to his wife, who turned out to be Cyd Charisse. Now that was glamorous. One night a few years ago, my wife and I were at the after party of the Comedy awards at the Comedy Store in Los Angeles. Coming in, I was introduced to Richard Pryor, who was in a wheelchair by then. He was drinking something very slowly through a straw. Later, we were chatting with Bill Maher and the actor Jeffrey Tambor, when who should wedge his way into our little foursome but Eric Idle of Monty Python fame. When we left, my wife asked me why I had been so quiet in the group, and I said I was afraid if I opened my mouth, the only thing that would come out was, "IT'S ERIC FUCKING IDLE! I'M TALKING TO ERIC FUCKING IDLE!" I will allow myself some kudos here, since one thing a comedian is rarely able to do is keep his big mouth shut.

I have worked in bars, clubs, hotel banquet rooms, college cafeterias (which I don't recommend), churches, Elks lodges, ski lodges, school auditoria, curling rinks, hockey arenas, theatres, cruise ships, lounges, TV soundstages, outdoor amphitheatres, casinos, malls, hospitals, restaurants, and private homes. I started in Toronto in 1980, in what might be called the golden age of Canadian standup. There were only three clubs that paid money back then. Two in Toronto and one in Montreal. I learned my business through watching others and painful, repeated failure onstage. The red light of our title was the little reminder for the comedian. It was placed in various locations, always where the comedian could see it but the audience, or most of the audience, could not. It always had the same meaning. Time's up, wrap it up, you're done, get off. Later it was used as a timing device, as in, "Give me a three minute light, or a five minute light." It wasn't always red, either, and most comedians refer to it simply as "The light." The steam whistle, the school bell, the signal that the fun is over, time to start waiting for the next show.

I don't think standup comedy is an art. Art has no time limit, no language restrictions, no light that says it's over. Comedy is a skill, a craft, a series of formulas and techniques. It can approach art, some nights when you go into a setup without knowing what the punch line will be and you come out on the other side with a big laugh and the thrill of surviving the jump. Maybe. Art affects everyone differently. I once saw a Cezanne painting at an exhibition and was very impressed by it. It moved me. Later, standing in front of another painting on the other side of the room, I glanced back to it and saw it completely differently. And again after that I saw it, this time from two rooms away, and again it was different. If comedy is to work, it must strike all audience members the same way. You can't really leave a joke open to interpretation. You can, but the laughs will be difficult to hear. After a bad show, one comedian I knew said, "Thanks very much, folks. It's been a real pleasure up here listening for you." Cezanne never had to worry about that, the lucky bastard. Although I suspect he might have had his own problems.

Listening is a crucial aspect of the job. How a joke sounds both rhythmically and alliteratively is most important. Why is 'keepsake' funnier than 'souvenir'? I'll give you a hint: it's the 'k' sound. Why is he funny and I'm not? How do I follow this guy? At a corporate show in Edmonton once I had to follow Andrew Grose, a fine comedian with several hours of good material on marriage and its peculiarities, a subject I have a solid hour on as well. Andrew's corporate set is predominantly marriage based, and I wasn't really thinking about that when I sailed into my marriage stuff about fifteen minutes into my set. The laughs got noticeably thin after a couple of minutes and I realized what was going on. "By the way," I asked, "Did Andrew talk about marriage at all?" This got a good laugh and I seguéed into other topics. A small mistake that I was able to correct. I should have been listening to Andrew's show.

Perhaps the most telling aspect of the job, the most enticing thing, is that you cannot share it. When you bomb, you take the blame, when you kill, you get the credit. It's the double hook. Being alone in front of an audience can be daunting (thank God, or everybody'd want to do it) for most people. The comedian sees this as a plus. It's the ultimate individual sport. There's no coach, no ensemble, no backup, no net. Karl Wallenda, the great tightrope walker, said, "Life is on the wire. The rest is waiting." He could have been talking about comedy. We're all just waiting for the next show. Of course, when we bomb, it doesn't usually result in broken bones or paralysis or death, though it sometimes feels that way.

You may think you want to be a comic. I applaud that notion, but I caution you that it means you must live the job. It must occupy you fully for at least the first three years. You have to do as many shows as you can, wherever you can, and tinker constantly with your ideas and perceptions. You need to love travelling, love being alone, love being away from your friends (if indeed, you have any). You will have enormous problems with your girlfriend or boyfriend, because you're always on the road. You'll worry a lot about your next job, your next joke, your next meal. My wife recently said she liked it when I was away for a week, and then home for a week. A good rhythm, she thought. She doesn't like it when I'm away for five or six weeks at a time, or when I'm home for that long a period. After the third week I get squirrelly. What's next? When's my agent going to call? Doesn't anyone want me anymore? I didn't take offence at what my wife said. I love her. We've been married for fourteen wonderful years. Nineteen total.

The following tale deals with my life from roughly age twenty, when I started at Yuk Yuks, to age thirty-one, when I did the Tonight Show for the first time. It is, I am hopeful, a classic scenario. Boy gets the comedy bug; boy becomes comic; boy kills; boy bombs; boy bombs again, and again, and again; boy tries to figure it out; boy gets better; boy gets pretty good; boy meets girl; boy sleeps with girl after show; boy cheats on girl; boy loses girl; boy gets the Tonight Show; boy never grows up. The end.

This book came about as a result of another book. A few years back, Andrew Clark, a Toronto writer, penned a history of Canadian standup called Stand And Deliver. Quite a lot of it had to do with the rise of Yuk Yuks Komedy Kabaret in Toronto. The most fascinating thing for me was the odd omission of John Wing. When I bought the book, the first thing I did was turn to the index to see if my name appeared. It did not. (I make no apologies for my ego here.) I figured that since I lived in Los Angeles, he hadn't travelled that far to interview me. But upon reading it, I discovered that he had come to L.A. and interviewed all the guys from my group except me. This made me angry, since I was one of only three guys from the original group of comedians at Yuks to do the Tonight Show with Johnny Carson. I was the one most people thought would never make it. My story was surely among the most interesting. (Another thing you have to believe with a passion to do this job.) Plus, I remembered quite a lot from the eighties in Toronto, despite the fact that I was stoned for virtually the entire decade. I could have told him about the New Year's Eve that Frank Van Keekan went onstage completely nude. About the night Lou Eisen and I snuck into Maple Leaf Gardens to watch the closed circuit broadcast of the Ray Leonard-Marvin Hagler fight. The night I accidentally kicked over a tray full of marijuana that Simon Rakoff was preparing to roll into a restorative joint. How he's never forgiven me for it to this day. I could tell you some stories.

But of course I must thank Andrew for his careless exclusion of me. Without it I wouldn't have been inspired to write my history of our time. As best I remember it. Some names have been changed to protect the writer from scurrilous libel actions. Some lines may have been garbled in their translation in my head. If I changed someone's line, my only defence is to say I probably made it better. Of course, what I didn't expect in looking back at my life from twenty to thirty was how embarrassing, how truly cringe-worthy a lot of it was. Nostalgia can be very sweet, but real reflection is appropriately stomach-turning. If I had any real sense, I wouldn't have touched it with a ten foot pole. Luckily, I have an eleven foot pole.

John Wing Jr.
27 May, 2008
Sarnia, Ontario

A man who was down on his luck was walking down a street one day when he passed a circus setting up for a show that evening. A sign said MAN WANTED. The man had not eaten in two days, and decided to apply for this job, whatever it was. He went to the boss's trailer, and was soon hired and told to report to the elephant cages. The job would not pay much, but he would have enough to eat and a place to sleep. On the way to the elephant cages, the man figured he'd probably be shovelling elephant shit. But no, the man who shovelled the elephant shit was his boss. He was told that the elephants had to take their dumps every night before the show, so they wouldn't be pooping all over the tent. The man's job was to make sure each elephant took a shit before every show. To that end, he was given a long, thick broomstick and told to go down the line of elephants and shove the stick up the rectum of each one, roll it around a bit, and then pull it out and step away fast, lest he be drowned in the cascade. When he was done, he could report to the meal wagon. The man used the thought of that meal wagon as he went down the line, inserting the broomstick carefully in each elephant's ass, rooting it around and then jumping back as the shit came down. Finally, he reached the eighth and last elephant, who was an elderly graybeard with cracked skin that the circus kept now as an alternate. The animal was asleep on his feet as the man approached. The man was repeating to himself again and again that after this one, he would eat. After this one, he would eat. He set the broomstick in place, and then slammed it way up the elephant's ass. The elephant's eyes opened wide and he turned to the man and said, "How's the crowd?"

TRAVEL DAY

AFTER TWO days of waiting around, I finally leave the ship, *Vision Of The Seas,* in Ochos Rios, Jamaica. I should have left two days ago, in Cozumel. The job was done. But my ticket was booked for yesterday in Grand Cayman. Fine. Then we couldn't even land in Grand Cayman because the swell was too high, so that went by the way. Now it's Jamaica. Instead of having a day at home in Los Angeles to unpack and pack, I have to go straight to Detroit armed with Caribbean clothing.

It is March sixth, 2001. Tuesday. I am a stand-up comedian who works, these days, mostly cruise ships. In three months, I will have been a comedian for twenty-one years. The last nineteen years have been spent, with one six-month interruption, on the road. Comedy clubs, bars, strip clubs, dives, parties, corporate events, ships, TV shows, etcetera. I have travelled across the continent and back, up and down, diagonally, every which way, but I've never been in Jamaica before.

Robert, the ship's production manager, walks with me down the dirty pier to the customs office. "Jamaica is the only place I've ever been where everyone you see is doing nothing," he says. "You've never been to Sarnia," is my catchy reply. Customs is a formality. Any weapons or drugs? Not today, thank you.

My cabdriver heaves my bag into the back of a new-ish minivan and I get into the shotgun seat. On the left. Steering wheel to my right. A first for me, and somewhat disconcerting for the first few minutes. We pick up two other passengers, a couple, at a horrid looking, squalid little condo complex a few blocks away and then we are off to Montego Bay. I hum the song of the same name that was briefly popular when I was a boy. I have been told the trek from Ochos Rios to the Montego Bay airport takes two and a half hours. I've been told it's close to 120 miles. As we leave the main part of town a sign says: MONTEGO BAY – 87.

The scent is fruity and it's not too drippingly hot yet at 10:30 a.m. Or as they say in the U.S. 10:30 a.m. in the morning. You know, so there's no confusion. The radio station is playing a cricket match between Ghana, whom the driver refers to as "those bastards", and Jamaica, whom he calls, "de bes', mon". Ghana is batting and has 270 for eight, which seems like a lot. The announcers never get more excited than a dog at midday and compare every single play to ones they saw thirty or forty years ago.

The road around the island mostly hugs the coast, and there are stretches where the Atlantic laps right up to it, although not too powerfully because of the outlying reef. We drive fast in spurts, then slowly, as the road turns from shiny blacktop to potholed gravel pit. Potholes with trout swimming in them, as Larry Horowitz used to say. We pass Catholic and Evangelical churches, but the main religion here seems to be tailgating. Our cabby drives like a maniac, and I'm grateful that I have two handrails where I sit, frozen with fear as he barrels up behind someone, coming within a few millimeters of a rear end collision, honks a couple of times and pulls out to pass. The passes are normally done at places in which I was taught *never* to pass. Going uphill, around curves, *with cars clearly visible in the oncoming lane.* The honk appears to be a universal signal to both the car being passed and the car about to hit us as we do. It says, "Slow down, you idiot." Or perhaps, "You idiot, don't kill us." Or even "Oooohhh*shit!*" Finally, after about 20 minutes of playing Dodgem, a sign says, DIVIDED HIGHWAY AHEAD. I breath of sigh of relief. We come to the divided highway, which lasts all of maybe fifteen seconds, and we're back to tailgating in the two-lane. Except this two-lane doesn't even have a stripe down the middle. As the divided highway begins and ends, another sign appears. MONTEGO BAY – 100. Uh-oh. Something's wrong here.

The vegetation seems stunningly dense. We pass a field of grass taller than me, followed by a perfectly manicured, fresh cut field. The scents drift in and out. Cut grass and salt air. A sign says HORSEBACK RIDEING, and I think of Ring Lardner. That's how he would have spelled it. A brown hawk settles on a low-lying branch to watch us pass. The trees are gnarly and in full leaf. I must get a book about the indigenous trees of this island. We pass a large grove of cactus, the only one so far, and the skin of the plants is bleached taupe by the sun, which is up in full force now. The Chukka Cove Polo Club comes into view and I think I've heard that Prince Charles has played polo here, though why I would care is anyone's guess. The cricket match drones on, Ghana still batting, amazingly still 270 for eight. Time does seem to be standing still today. The match will probably still be going when I come back in three weeks.

We're getting into poorer areas now. A ramshackle tin roof town appears. The little vending shacks along the road are mostly boarded up, the houses behind them not much bigger and no nicer. We pass a lot of half-built, or half-destroyed, concrete houses, ridiculously small and pathetic, the wires sticking up as though more will be done. As we pass through the centre of this ghetto a sign offers one-acre lots, ocean OR mountain views, starting at $27,000, U.S. funds. No wonder Noel Coward moved here. I keep looking up to see if his house is visible in the hills.

The Bauxite-By-The-Sea plant looms up on the ocean side. A bunch of giant, rusty vats with conical tops. No humans anywhere. There are people you do see, but they're not doing anything. All along the highway there are women, in white shirts and blue pants, standing by the road, looking up one way and down the other. Roasting in the heat waiting for what? A bus? We never see even one all the way to Montego Bay. Our driver comes up behind a cop car, again missing the bumper by angstroms, honks, and speeds past him at 110 klicks. The cop never looks at us.

Muttering, "those dirty *bastards*", the driver changes to a reggae station. After three or four songs, or maybe just one long really boring song, the DJ does a phone interview with a Canadian (Jamaican-born) reggae star. He won a Juno award last night for best reggae album. They chat about the awards, held in Toronto, and the news of my old city cheers me up immensely. It also tips me to the road sign problem. I ask the driver if the signs are in miles or kilometers. His speedometer reads klicks. He says the whole island is in the process of switching over from miles to klicks. That explains that. This scintillating bit of byplay is the only conversation among the four of us for the entire 120-mile, 90-kilometer, whatever drive.

And on we go. Yellow sand beaches crammed with brightly coloured fishing launches. A burned out church. An old stone building at the entrance to a small harbour that looks like it took some cannon fire a couple of hundred years back. Many resorts. *Half Moon, The Rose Club,* etc. The RED STRIPE BEER signs outnumber the DON'T DRINK AND DRIVE signs three to one. In Falmouth, a sign on a building says FOREVER YOUNG CHEMICALS. A Hollywood presence at last.

We arrive at the airport a little after noon. The temperature is 31 degrees Celsius. Humidity ten zillion. The airport is probably one of the largest in the Caribbean. A lot of shops that, amazingly, don't sell anything worth a damn. I hump it to the gate early and inquire as to a rest room. It's all the way back where I came in. This airport has only one rest room, sir. I hump it all the way back to the goddamn rest room. The urinal is placed so high I have to pee up to get it in. No paper towels, but an air hand dryer my lungs could beat. I board early and can't stop thinking about Toronto. Although the place I think about doesn't really resemble the Toronto of today. I lived there from 1980 to 1988. Back then I wanted to be a comedian.

A friend of mine recently said to me, "You know, my parents told me to get my degree so I'd have something to fall back on in case show business didn't work out. They never even mentioned what it would be like if show business *did* work out." So for those of you who are interested, here's a look back and a little primer on how one gets this job. And how one keeps this job. In short, *When the Red Light Goes On, Get Off.*

My father always told me to avoid certain professions. The law, his calling, was one of them. "Don't be a lawyer," he'd say. "You never know where your next meal is coming from." He didn't think much of being a musician, either. "You'll be on the road all your life." I became a comedian. So I never know where my next meal is coming from and I've been on the road for over twenty years.

BEGINNINGS: 1980

I GREW UP in Sarnia, the second of five children, and as first son, I was named John Malcolm Wing, Jr. My parents encouraged all of their children to be artistic, and as a result I have a sister who's a playwright, a brother who teaches high school English and drama while acting occasionally and writing novels in his spare time, a sister who is an opera soprano diva and also teaches voice, and a brother who has written everything from political speeches to record reviews. Growing up together, we were competitive and grew somewhat sharp-witted around the Lord Rapier, my father, and the saint, my mother. I am capable of appearing to be a nice guy because of what I inherited from Mom, and also capable of skewering anyone with deliberate cruelty thanks to the German-English-Irish genes I got from Dad. For the job I picked, not a bad combination.

I lived nineteen years in Sarnia, longer than either my older sister, who left for finishing school at seventeen, and my immediately younger brother, who left for private school (five-year full scholarship) at fourteen. After two years of fun at the University of Windsor, I returned home for my twenty-first summer. It was 1980. Dad secured me a job cleaning out cabin cruisers for a boat company. I had never been fired from a job before I worked there, and I would be fired from that and every job thereafter. They caught me sleeping in one of the boats one afternoon and I was summarily dismissed. Even my fabulous excuse, mentioning that I'd stayed up all night the previous evening, didn't change their minds. Unbelievable.

I had stayed up all night because my college friend, John Richards, was playing a bar gig (singing) at The Wheels Inn in Chatham and had invited me to drive up and catch the show. After the show he and I caught up until six a.m. He wanted me to come to Toronto, where he was living, and join his band, The Pontoon Brothers, as the drummer. The whole band was living in a house and there was an extra room for me. Driving back to Sarnia early in the morning, slapping my face as hard as I could every few minutes to stay awake, I wondered how I would get my father to agree to this.

Of course, he agreed right away. Looking back, it doesn't seem as surprising as it did then. I had just been fired from a job a retarded guy could do. I was aimless and generally lazy. Maybe he thought that getting me out into the shit would be the best thing for me. He had advice about being in the band and said that if it didn't work out over the summer, he'd pay the full whack for my third year at Windsor. An amazing, you-have-to-take-it offer. I took it. Phoned John and told him to expect me. Packed whatever was meaningful and booked a train.

I took a cab to the station, as I recall. Standing on the platform, having a cigarette before boarding, I saw Dad pull up in the big grey Mercury. We had a cigarette together. He asked if I had any money, and I said I'd saved close to $200. He smiled, the way I do now when my nine-year-old tells me that Britney Spears' Dance Camp is only $1200 a week. Dad reached into his wallet and handed me $300. A fortune. We hugged and kissed on the platform. He probably realized, though I didn't, that this was it. I would never return as anything but a visitor. I boarded, found a seat and waved. He waved for a while as the train pulled out and then turned toward the parking lot. He said many years later he was very frightened for me. He couldn't have been any more frightened than I was.

IT'S PAINFUL to think about the 20-year-old child I was when I left home. I spent the first night in London, staying with a girl pianist I had the hots for. We went to see *A Clockwork Orange* at the local rep house, and just as I don't recommend seeing *Apocalypse Now* when you want to unwind after a tough final exam, I don't think seeing *Clockwork* does much for your sexual prowess. I had a tiny bit of prowess, virtually no knowledge, and the movie spooked me, so nothing much happened that night.

Arriving in Toronto the next afternoon, I made my way to the band house at Coxwell and Gerrard streets in the east end of town. Aside from John, there were three other people in residence. Dave McLaren, called "Moot" by everyone, a stout, big-headed fellow who looked like a bouncer. Cathy Bertolo, a Sault Ste. Marie girl, our designated person-with-a-real-job, was nice and fun. She worked for an insurance company. There was a guy named Wino. His real name was Steve, I think, but John had told him one day that he looked like a wino, and from then on, everyone had called him Wino. John was that way. He had given Dave his nickname, and he started calling me "Morty" for no discernible reason.

The house was a typical Toronto row house . As you came in, the stairway was dead ahead, double living room on the left, and the kitchen behind that. The upstairs was L-shaped, with the washroom at the top of the stairs and three bedrooms along the hallway. There was a rickety stairway to the third floor, which had one room. My room.

The news upon my arrival wasn't good. The band had folded that morning. The lead singer and rhythm guitarist had taken a powder. As soon as I hit the door, we re-formed. John, lead guitar, would take over on vocals, and with Moot on bass and me on drums, we would become a 'power trio'. The Police were getting hot then, and Rush was the biggest live act in the country, so we would be in good company. We went down to the basement and rehearsed a few songs. I was rusty as hell but they guys didn't seem to mind. John took me out to a thrift store late in the afternoon and I bought a night table, a chair, and some bedding for my room.

Then, I was at loose ends. Everyone else in the house had something planned. In the back of my mind I had been thinking about this comedy club that had been getting some attention the last year or so. I had heard about it in the last month of school. It was called Yuk Yuks. I decided to attend a show and see what it was all about.

To backtrack a bit here, I grew up with comedy all around me. Making my father laugh was the general pastime of all his children. He had a sudden, powerful laugh that betrayed real happiness, and it was addictive. We were comedy junkies. In the bookshelves were P.G. Wodehouse, S.J. Perelman, Ring Lardner, Max Shulman, Guy Gilpatric, Mark Twain. Dad could quote huge chunks out of any book with any of those names. Word perfect; funny as hell. On Sunday mornings for

HOOKED: *I'd always felt at home on stage, and if you include lying, I'd been a performer all my life.*

years we would watch Abbott and Costello movies. Dad was a major fan of the only two comedy teams I ever saw, other than Nichols and May, where both people could play straight or be funny: Laurel and Hardy, and Gleason and Carney. Any one of them could literally put my father on the floor with the smallest thing. Carney shooting his cuffs, Gleason bugging his eyes out, Laurel doing *anything,* Hardy falling down with that pitiful yelp of his. A great admirer of Danny Kaye, my father would call us in to watch *The Inspector General* or *The Court Jester.* He had seen Danny Kaye live. We would watch comedians on Ed Sullivan, the first one I recall well being Scoey Mitchell, who told the funniest joke I had ever heard up to that time. We were Monty Python fanatics and Dad was a big fan of Benny Hill as well. I never liked Benny all that much, but I'd watch him just to see Dad laugh. It was that much fun. From the highbrow snobbishness of Perelman to the pratfalls and puns of the Marx Brothers and Benny Hill, we had everything.

Of course, the idea of being a stand-up comedian simply wasn't practical. This was Canada. I suppose it was in the back of my mind that night as I went to Yuk Yuks for the first time. I had tried almost all the other forms of entertainment. Acted in plays, played guitar in bars, speech contests, bands, etcetera. I didn't know yet that they all lacked something that stand-up had in spades.

Yuk Yuks Komedy Kabaret was at the corner or Bay and Yorkville street, in the basement of an odd sort of restaurant mall at the bad end of impossibly trendy Yorkville Street. I paid four dollars to get in and sat myself at a small table near the sound booth. The trapezoidal room seemed very small, perhaps sixty feet by forty-five, the stage centred at the long end. The ceiling was quite low. On the two-foot-high stage, your head would hit the ceiling if you jumped. Except for the multicoloured Yuk Yuks logo on the wall behind the stage, everything in the room was black. The walls, the ceiling, the carpet, the tables, the chairs and the waitresses uniforms. There was a small curtain to the right of the stage and from there the comedians entered. You didn't have to walk through the audience to get to the stage, which was a nice touch, something I've rarely if ever seen anywhere else. It made it seem more professional. More showbiz. The low ceiling made for excellent sound, the sound of the laughs coming up at you. In a high-ceilinged room, the laughs have to go all the way to the top and then back down to you, making them more difficult to time properly. The all black motif made it a room with no distractions. Even the bar was in the back and well hidden. It remains the most perfectly crafted and appointed comedy room I've ever seen.

The host that night was Martin Waxman, more a writer than a comedian per se. The show included Ralph Benmergui, Lou Dinos, Larry Horowitz, Mike MacDonald, all of whom were uniquely impressive, though widely different in style. Ralph was sophisticated, above it all. *"You must realize that television is brought to you by people who expect you to believe that nobody ever screwed on Gilligan's Island. I mean, come on! Ginger, Mary Ann, Mrs. Howell.......okay, maybe not Mrs. Howell. If I get that horny I'll swim to shore."* Lou was more ethnic in his approach, talking about his heritage. *"I'm Greek. My parents came to this country so they could speak Macedonian."* Larry was smooth and technically perfect with observational humour. The little things amused him. *"Did you ever see someone clean out their ear with their finger and then they look at it? What the hell do they expect to find? 'Hey, Lotto Canada tickets...'"* Mike was a purely physical comedian, a Gumby of movement and rage. He did a piece about playing Monopoly for the first time in years. *"It's embarrassing to own one of those shitty properties. You know, Baltic and Mediterranean. What's even more embarrassing is to have houses on those properties. People land on them: 'What's the rent? Two dollars?? Here's ten, fuck off."*

After a most exhilarating hour came the headliner, Lawrence Morgenstern. A big, blustery comedian, whose style and swagger made him seem older than he was. He came out bursting with energy, laying out inventive bits about television. He was a TV junkie. Somehow, though, it just wasn't working on this night. Perhaps his style was grating after the first four guys, maybe we were tired, maybe he didn't read us right, but for the first 20 minutes of his show, Lawrence couldn't get a roll going. There were intermittent laughs, but nothing big and nothing to build on. Finally, he did his Star Trek bit, which included an argument between Mr. Spock and Dr. McCoy. Lawrence had always wanted Spock to bust out and give some anger back to McCoy, just once.

McCOY: *Damn ya Spock! Ya long-eared green-blooded Vulcan queer! If I want your advice I'll ask for it!*

SPOCK: *Doctor, it would seem to be what you humans call 'that time of the month' for you.*

Then Lawrence reached under his left arm with his right hand, simulating masturbation as though his penis came out of his ribcage, and sneered: *"Suck my Vulcan cock!"*

This produced a monster laugh. The first real one he'd received. And it made him angry, taking 20 minutes to get a real laugh. He turned on us.

"Oh, so *that's* what you like, is it? Not the well written stuff, the highbrow. No, you prefer the *cocksucking* stuff!"

After that outburst, there were no more laughs. The audience made a decision, and for the remaining forty-five minutes of his show, we silently watched him go insane at the fact that he couldn't get a laugh. He was supposed to do forty-five minutes and he did sixty-five because he couldn't stand leaving it without getting at least one. They had to turn the stage lights out to get him off. He got the hint. "Goodnight, you *bastards.*" Martin Waxman came back on, a bit nonplussed, to say the least, and ended the show. As we filed out into the small courtyard looking up onto Bay street, Lawrence came out another door and started screaming at us.

"What the fuck is *wrong* with you people!?! Do you have *any idea* how funny I am?? ANY IDEA AT ALL!?!"

It was surreal, or it least it appears that way now in my memory. I remember wondering if all comedy shows were like this.

A WEEK LATER, on a Saturday night I went again. A weekend show was different from a week night. Week nights were easygoing and relaxed, nobody was too dressed up, there were regulars. Weekends were dress up and spend money, have dinner and see the show. There were only two sets before the headliner, and the host was Mark Breslin, the owner of Yuks. He was introduced by a video. There were two TV sets mounted high on the walls on either side of the stage and they came on to reveal Mark sitting backstage talking on the phone while one of the waitresses licked his shoes clean. Dismissing the caller with a "you'll never work in this town again!" sort of kiss off,

Mark produced a needle kit and pretended to shoot up very realistically. (I had to turn away every time I saw it, and writing about it makes my arm throb.) His eyes would roll back and he would keen a bit, then dismiss the bootlicker, put on his jacket and head down the dark corridor that led to the stage. And the intro would begin from the sound booth:

"Good evening, ladies and gentlemen, and welcome to Yuk Yuks Komedy Kabaret, here in the heart of pretentious Yorkville. We have a fabulous show for you tonight, starring our featured act, Mike MacDonald! And now, would you welcome to the stage your host, the founder of Yuk Yuks, and a really mean, fucked-up, little Jew, Mr. Mark Breslin!"

The stage lights would blaze and Mark would appear, impeccably dressed. A perfect suit, shoes shined to a high gloss, handkerchief just so. He was, unlike most owner performers (and you know who you are), a real comedian. He had a real act which he wrote himself, mostly, and great timing. He knew all the hosting tricks and he had the blackest sense of humour I've ever come across. Mine is merely black. His is coal-dust-in-the-lung black. He once told me that he was so dirty and dark because it helped the shows. "Once they see me, nobody I bring on can *ever* shock or offend them." While that wasn't literally true, because Mark often brought in headliners who were intended to shock, it was generally true.

I was seated at one of the two front centre tables that night, the result of being alone at a sold-out show and that being the only seat. A woman sat right in front of me and Mark opened the show by talking to her and then mock flogging her with the mike cord, calling her a dirty little girl. The audience ate it up. Shawn Thompson, possibly the best looking comedian who ever lived, came out first and picked me for his Find-The-Condom-In-The-Guy's-Wallet bit, hauling me up onstage to be embarrassed. He asked me what I did for a living, and I said I was an aspiring comedian. He smiled and said, "Oh yeah? Bull*shit!*" It got a jolting laugh which felt good even though I had given the straight line. Shawn didn't have the sharpest or most original act, but he used every ounce of his ability and I only saw him bomb once in eight years. And I never saw him do an indifferent or medio-cre set. He murdered every time except that one time when he bombed. He was performing at a late-night show for actors and the-atre people, and his clubby, blond-guy-doing-Catskills style was some-thing they'd all seen before and weren't impressed with. But I'm get-ting ahead of myself.

The headliner that night was Mike MacDonald. It was the first time I saw Mike do his hour. I probably saw him more than two hun-dred times in the next eight years and he was simply the best live act I've ever seen. He could make you forget where you were. The show would end and you'd look around and think, "Oh. I'm in a comedy club." And that's not an exaggeration. Mike's style was to tell you the joke, which was his setup, and then to physically *show* you the joke, which was his punchline. He would tell of going to the bank and the maze they made you go through to get to the tellers. This was pre-ATM, of course. The laughs came with his stiff-legged, arms akimbo walk through that maze. All the comedians got laughs, of course, but Mike's were different. He had a way of sustaining laughter. The last 20-25 minutes of his show, which included his signature piece, called "My Rock 'n Roll Fantasy", the laughter seemed almost continuous.

Mike just controlled the volume, turning up when he wasn't talking and dialing it down again when he was. Watching him was a glimpse of how transcendent stand-up could be, and I suspect that sounds pretentious, but I was young and Mike's virtuosity thrilled me and made me determined.

I talked to the club manager afterward, and he told me to come down on Monday and get my name on the amateur list. He was sizing me up as he gave me the info. Years later he told me that I didn't look like much competition for anyone. He said he'd see to it that I got on the list and he'd make sure I got in free. I didn't pay to get into a comedy show again for seven years. It was truly a night of firsts and lasts. It was the first time anybody ever asked me what I did for a living, and the last time I ever sat up front.

I showed up early the next Monday and the first person I saw in the club was Mike MacDonald, listening on headphones to a tape of his Sunday night show. When he took the headphones off I went over and told him how much I had enjoyed his Saturday show. He was very polite and we chatted for a moment, which surprised me, because he was a big, square-headed guy who looked much older than he was and he had an aura of violence about him. *Stay away or I'll fuck you up* emanated from him quite clearly. But when you got inside that, he was a pleasant enough fellow. He told me to tape every show, which was the single best piece of advice I ever got from anyone about the job. Watching him was always a lesson. He was the number one guy in Toronto. Everyone else was playing in the second division. And he worked like a dog. (I noted the correlation.) He taped all his shows. Audio, and then later video. He wanted only to get better, get funnier.

Not for a TV show deal or a movie deal, just because being funny was just the best damn thing to be.

My first Monday night fell on the 30th of June, 1980. I had started writing jokes, of a sort, in the last few months of that school year, when I'd first heard about the comedy club in Toronto. The Saturday before my debut, I did my so-called set at the house on Coxwell for a few people, and it seemed to go very well.

The rules were simple. You had five minutes onstage, and when you got the light – a flashing red light on a ceiling beam about half across the room – it meant get off. Not do another minute or so, not wait until your next laugh. Just *get off the stage, now.* If you dallied, or worse, got no laughs at all for the first three minutes or so, they would turn off the stage lights and the mike until you left. This ignominious ending never happened to me, but there were nights it could have. Easily.

The five-minute rule was hotly debated and despised by the amateurs. The pros always gave the same old line: "If you can't make them laugh in five minutes, you can't make them laugh in ten." We resented this aphorism, no doubt because it was true. I would even amend it to one minute now. Watching the odd amateur night these days, I can often tell by the way someone walks to the stage whether they'll be funny or not. Failing that, the first line is an infallible reporter.

My set at the house ran six and a half minutes, but I wasn't concerned. In fact, I was eerily confident. I invited John and Moot to come with me, something Lou Dinos told me later he would never have done. "Hey man, what if you'd sucked?" Maybe at age twenty embarrassment isn't what it is at forty. My slot was horrible. I went fifteenth out of eighteen. I was the newest guy so I got a poor spot. But it was a bad night for comedians. Nobody except the host, Simon Rakoff, was getting any response. Simon got a lot of laughs out of how badly everyone was faring.

"Let's hear it for Josh, and if you're interested in following Josh's career, he'll be taking the Bay bus home."

"I hesitate to bring this next guy up because he's really funny and it might throw you guys off."

And then I was standing in the dark, one-person-wide corridor, waiting to be introduced. The rush of taking the stage was palpable. It must be something like jumping out of a plane or off a bridge on a bungee cord. Here we go into the black.

I actually did eight minutes that night. And everything, from the first line on, got big laughs. *Big* laughs. It was almost unimaginable. The set was really dirty, naturally. One of the hallmarks of the amateur is filthy material, as it's the easiest way to get laughs. I did Neil Young singing a song about fellatio. I did a bit about whacking off, the idea stolen from chapter two of Portnoy's Complaint. (Another hallmark of the amateur is unabashed plagiarism). I ad libbed. I felt the roll, the astounding confidence, the belief that everything you say is going to be funny. I closed with an impression of John F. Kennedy at his inaugural, stoned out of his mind. I stole that one from a college friend. And the laughs came. They rose up and showered me, fell back and I went chasing after them. I came off to loud applause and went sailing down the dark hallway to the green room. Lou Dinos was there with a big grin on his face. I nodded to him, suddenly sweaty, and headed out the door. He stopped me.

"Listen to that," he said, referring to the applause, which was still going on.

"So what?" I replied. Lou looked shocked. "They applaud for everyone," I said. "They laughed for me. That's what's important." To a degree, I still think that's true.

My set caused a bit of a sensation, and I was invited back the next week. Usually, because there were so many amateurs vying for spots, you could only do two Mondays a month. It was rumoured that I might get off Amateur Night right away, once Mark Breslin saw me and gave me the rubber stamp. Only one comedian had ever gone straight from his first Monday to regular nights, but I thought it would be simple. Kill again, get promoted, and the career would move from there. What's to worry about? The fact that I might not have idea number one about what I was doing never entered my mind. It rarely did in those days.

The next Monday came, and I was back in the green room, nervous and excited. A bunch of regulars were there. Lawrence Morgenstern was holding court, telling the story of the *horrible* audience he had encountered on the Thursday night of his feature week. The show I saw. Luckily I was smart enough not to voice my own opinion. Lawrence's version was holding, however, until Ralph Benmergui, lying on the couch as though he were the weariest man alive, said that the audience wasn't that bad. He'd done a funny set for the same crowd. "Face it Lawrence," he said, "the set was the low point of your career." Lou noticed me and introduced me around, saying how great my set had been last Monday and that I would probably be promoted tonight. Everyone said hello except Ralph. He was unimpressed, to put it mildly. And he was right.

I went up that night in a prime spot, with a great intro, did the same set, and got nothing. *N-O-T-H-I-N-G*. The energy was much different, I wasn't as juiced on adrenaline, whatever it was. I did not get even one laugh. I was suddenly the little boy who'd been found out. Hanging my head, staring at the guitar pick I nervously rolled between my fingers, accepting their rebuke, which was worse than any screaming harangue. They just sat there, silently hoping I'd be done soon. I fled the stage after five minutes and was sitting in the back hallway behind the club when Mark Breslin came up to me, smiling a rueful smile.

"I'm afraid you're not ready yet," he said. Something he would say to me many times over the next two years. I walked all the way home that night, thirteen subway stops, wallowing in my sadness, something I'd always been good at.

That night is the reason I became a comedian. If it had gone as planned and I'd graduated to regular nights, I might still be a comedian, but not necessarily. Bombing that completely was the real impetus. I'd spent a week flying high after the first set, convinced I was really good at this. I'd always felt at home on stage, and if you include lying, I'd been a performer all my life. Mostly it had come naturally and easily. But the pure humiliation of July 7th, 1980 forced me to admit that I was really going to have to work at this. Work my way back to the intoxicating sound of that first night. I didn't know it would take years, *years*, to get there, but it wouldn't have mattered. I was hooked.

It was an interesting summer. I had a place to live and an obsession. What could be sweeter? I looked for a job during the day and went to Yuk Yuks at night. It wasn't more than a month before John and Moot sat me down and fired me as the drummer in their band. I was too wrapped up in comedy to be serious about anything else. there were no hard feelings and probably sighs of relief at both ends, since I wasn't a great drummer. I continued to live at the house on Coxwell, now nicknamed, "The House Of The Damned" by John. I sold theatre subscriptions door to door for a while, and a more difficult profession I couldn't imagine. Those who didn't immediately order me off their property could always find reasons not to buy what I was selling. One guy told me I was hawking the wrong product and gave me an address where a better selling job could be found. I went to the place and applied. It was a job selling encyclopedias. Two nights later I went in to attend a seminar for hopeful salesmen. They gave us three hours of soft and hard sell techniques. Having nothing else to do, I paid attention for a while, and a question was suddenly put to me by the main speaker, probably hoping to rattle me. I gave the right answer with no hesitation and when it was over, they called me into the office and offered me the job. Being an idiot, I accepted. "Congratulations!" he boomed. "YOU'RE A SALESMAN!" It was Thursday night and I was told to report Monday morning.

All the way home to the House Of The Damned, I tried to find reasons to be happy about this job. I could find none. This seguéed into finding reasons not to go on Monday, but I couldn't find a good one there, either. John came to my rescue. He suggested I just not show up. "But they'll phone and then what'll I say?" John said he'd man the phone on Monday and if they phoned he'd tell them I was dead. He then gave a hysterical performance of a barely in control guy telling the encyclopedia boys I'd committed suicide.

"No, he's not coming in. No, he's not. He can't, okay? Why? You wanna know why? All right, he's DEAD! That's why. Okay? You happy now? He's dead! I don't know man....I DON'T KNOW!! He came home the other night, he was so happy. Christ, I never saw him so fucking happy. And then this morning we find him in the bathroom with his wrists slashed! So he won't be coming in! Got that? Great, pass it along."

Eventually I started playing guitar on Yonge Street for food and cigarette money. I found a perfect spot in front of the ScotiaBank (now gone) at the corner of Wellesley and Yonge. Wellesely subway station was right there, so there was constant foot traffic in both directions. The flow of people was so river-like that you only had to know one long song and one short one to play all day without anyone noticing your lack of repertoire. My parents came to visit and see what I'd blundered into. My father was very impressed that I was street singing, saying to me later that he figured if I could do that, I could do anything, and I'd be okay. My mother used the bathroom at the House Of The Damned, which impressed everyone.

The first day I played on Yonge Street I made ten dollars and a chunk of hash in four hours. I took the hash home and we had a little party. One day in the second week an old college friend came by and told me he was working for a great security company, and they were hiring right now. He gave me the address. I checked it out the next day and was hired in nothing flat. They gave me a uniform. Two nights after that they sent me on my first job. A night shift at a mall. I have no recollection of where it was, but I sat in a chair from midnight to eight a.m. on a Saturday and guarded the premises. I also had a major anxiety attack in the wee hours. *What am I doing? Is this my life? Is this what it's going to be?* My stomach ached and I couldn't stop the doubts. Everything was happening too fast or too slow.

Two days later I was assigned to a permanent (yeah right) post at the ManuLife Centre, a combination apartment complex and mall at Bay and Bloor. Two blocks from Yuk Yuks. Here I was one of many. We patrolled the mall, helped the tenants by opening their storage lockers, or occasionally throwing out their stalking lovers, and we wrote reports. Lots of reports. The three shifts were 11-7, 7-3, and 3-11. You did the same shift for two weeks at a time. I told the boss I liked the late night shift best, and since nobody else liked it much, I usually did it, freeing my evenings for Yuks and my days for sleep.

A few weeks after being hired at ManuLife, I found my own apartment downtown. I liked living with John and everyone at the House Of The Damned, but I was a lousy roommate. I had grown up having everything done for me by mother, so I didn't cook or clean much and I could barely do laundry. It never occurred to me, monumentally self-absorbed as I was, that this would be a problem. Then one night we were all hanging out in the living room doing an impromptu jam session when Cathy came in with a drawing she had just finished. She was a first-rate caricaturist. The drawing was a group portrait of all of us. There was John and Moot and Cathy and Wino, smiling. Behind the group was me, hanging by the neck until I was dead, a bag over my head. Everyone thought it was hilarious. I hope I wasn't too petulant about it but I probably was. I had always been hypersensitive and ill-tempered, a lethal combination if you expect to have friends. I knew I wasn't pulling my share, but it was now obvious that everyone knew I wasn't pulling my share. It wasn't long after that night that I found my own place. Easier to change your pub than your character.

I found a place on Homewood, a long two blocks between Carlton and Wellesley, ending at Wellesley Hospital, just east of Maple Leaf gardens. It was a furnished basement one-room with a tiny kitchen and a bathroom that wouldn't fit two people unless one of them was lying in the tub. The kitchen had a sink, a two-burner hot plate that took up the whole counter and a fridge the size of a hotel mini-bar. The main room was perhaps ten feet by seven, and I'm only guessing that by recalling that it was two long steps across the room from the door to the window, and three steps, short ones, from the kitchen door to the pullout couch on the far wall. It had a desktop and chair, a wardrobe and the sofa. When you pulled the bed out, the room virtually disappeared. The door wouldn't even open all the way when the bed was out. The couch was old, fraying green upholstery, the same disgusting colour as the carpet, which was older. The place smelled like old carpet. The window over the desktop looked up from ground level at an alley that was completely enclosed, so no sunlight ever penetrated my little haven. It was my first apartment and I adored it. It cost $160 a month and when I left two years later it cost $200. You couldn't rent a stoop in Toronto today for either price.

My father advanced me the $320 for first and last months' rent, the transaction signifying that I wouldn't be returning to school for the 80/81 season. Once I'd moved, I never returned to the House Of The Damned. A few weeks after I left, John phoned and invited me to see Bruce Springsteen at Maple Leaf Gardens. They had an extra ticket. We sat in the top row of the building and saw one hell of a rock concert, my first. A few months after that, I saw the latest incarnation of The Pontoon Brothers at a Queen Street pub, and I saw John in a tobacco shop about a year after I'd moved. He said he was planning to move to New Orleans, which he eventually did, re-forming the Pontoon Brothers as a comedy duo. We both ended up in Los Angeles at the end of the eighties, meeting again and restarting our friendship. John became a very successful screenwriter and won the screenplay award at the Cannes Film Festival in 2000 for *Nurse Betty*. But anyway.....back to me.

Always on the lookout for material, I walked the streets, eyes peeled for things I could make fun of. And a hook, a style. Something they'd remember me for. I heard Iggy Pop talking once about doing a show and he was drinking wine from a goblet during a slow song. Unbeknownst to him, the bottom of the glass broke off and he scraped his upper chest with the broken stem. "The crowd started going absolutely wild," he said, recalling it. "I looked down and my chest was just covered in blood. So that was when I started cutting myself onstage every night."

TO REGULAR NIGHTS: 1980/82

AN OLD FRIEND from Sarnia told me recently that after only a couple of times onstage, I informed him that comedy was what I wanted to do. I don't recall the conversation – I was probably stoned – but my actions prove it out. I lived for comedy. I wrote material all the time. Really bad material. "Is this funny?" became my mantra. I had a joke about Tolstoy writing War and Peace. *He would write about war on Mondays, Wednesdays, and Fridays, and he would write about peace on Tuesdays, Thursdays, and Saturdays. And on Sundays, he....watched football.* That was probably the first joke I wrote that kind of always worked and was all mine. I had another about dating, the first of a multitude on that subject. *She was telling me about her new boyfriend. "He's smarter than you, better looking, makes more money and he's so much better in bed than you." And I said, "Hey, if you break up, call me. I'll go out with him."* Later I wrote a better version of that joke. *My girlfriend is so into Burt Reynolds and I got a little jealous. I said, "So what? You take away the money, the good looks, the big cock, and what do you have?" And she said, "You."* My early Monday night sets usually had one or two laughs in them, just enough to ensure that the lights were never turned off.

But I did poorly, other than that. Week after week, I would promise myself that this time I would hit the stage with just the right personality and some fantastic new material. I would wear *this* outfit and

51

open with *that* joke, and *Whammo!* But there were no whammos. No whammos at all. Howie Wagman, who ran the club then, loves to tell me to this day how I was the only comic he was wrong about. He never thought I had a chance in hell. Recalling my sets of the period, it's easy to see why he thought so. I had a very slight jokewriting ability and some stage presence, and that was it. I wasn't a quick study, either. But I was there, at the club, every night. In the first two years, I might have missed between six and ten nights total.

I was an amateur for 21 months, which is a long time. There were guys who started long after me who got regular nights long before me. Pat Bullard was one. He was promoted after two amateur nights. Glen Foster started more than a year after me and we were promoted at around the same time.

There were three kinds of amateurs. Those who were good right off the bat. The naturals. Those who weren't very good at the start but you saw a spark and knew they'd improve, and those who weren't any good and never would be. I suppose there was a fourth group. The nutcases. One guy would spend his five minutes reading long 'roses are red, violets are blue' type poems all about Harold Ballard and the Leafs. He was pro-Leafs and anti-Ballard.

Al & George were among the naturals. Two Toronto boys who were the best comedy team Canada produced after Wayne and Shuster. There were other teams around then. Neil Ross and John Davies, The B.S. Factor, and a duo whose name escapes me now. They were mostly sketch performers. Al & George were a musical act, and their Amateur Night debut was the best I ever saw. They came out on that sleepy Monday, no one having ever heard of them. One of the easiest ways to spot amateurs is how they dress. Few of them ever realize that it's a show, and you should always look better than the audience. Al, concentration camp thin, came out wearing a very conservative single-breasted grey suit and tie. He looked like an undertaker. George had on a gold lamé jacket, ruffled shirt, black pants and winkle pickers, along with a most beatific smile that never left his face, and stage presence to burn. He toted a gorgeous guitar and immediately plugged in and started to play. He could strum as fast as Townshend, and they sang:

Hurry up and die, George Burns.
Hurry up and die, George Burns.
Hurry up and die. Join Gracie in the sky,
Why don't you hurry up and die George Burns.

It was a rousing, up tempo number, and when they exhorted us to sing along we all did. When the song ended, to wild applause, Al, who never smiled onstage, said, *"We just heard on the news that George Burns died at six o'clock this evening, so I hope you all feel good about laughing and clapping along."* After this laugh died down, he continued, *"No, I'm kidding. He didn't die. And we hope that Mr. Burns lives for a long time because, well, we don't have that much material."* Al & George were promoted to regular nights before their first set was over.

For most though, it wasn't like that. I remember four amateurs from that period. Josh Babyns, Vivian Holden, Garson Hoffmann, and Rick Grossman. None of them ever made it to regular nights. Josh simply wasn't funny. He was cute and personable, which got him exactly nowhere with the crowd. He was around for a year or so and then disappeared into some more reputable business. Garson was a tall, dark-featured guy who had one bit that always killed: a song about Chinese students at the University of Toronto that was as funny as it was racist. He had no other jokes that got a thing however, and he was gone by the time I was promoted. Vivian hung on for a while, but she never got any better than she was the first night I saw her. She had some mildly funny stuff about marriage and divorce and a how-males-pee-vs-how-females-pee bit, but her material and style never got over that hump.

Rick Grossman was a comedian like no other. He was a great guy. A genuinely nice, helpful person who always knew the best doctor for this, the best store for that. He even gave great directions, something I always needed. But he was the worst comedian God ever made. He couldn't make anything funny. He told some decent old jokes in his show and got no laughs. He had a couple of semi-original bits that got no laughs. Other comedians would suggest lines to him, he would do them and get no laughs. He stole some excellent material from U.S. comedians he saw on TV and got no laughs.

In Rick's defence, I'm not sure he ever knew he got no laughs. He had one bit that might have been funny. It was a story about being in his car, stopped at a light on a steep hill, with a full church bus ahead of him. The bus was festooned with stickers that read HONK IF YOU LOVE JESUS. While waiting for the light to change, the bus brakes began to fail and it started to slide back down the hill toward Rick's car. So he started honking. And all the people on the bus waved and smiled, because obviously he loved Jesus so much. Having set up a legitimately funny visual, as people would begin to laugh, Rick would scream out, "FUCK OFF, I'M JEWISH!!!" which spoiled the effect utterly. He literally stomped on the possibility of a laugh. It was, as we used to say, a-fucking-mazing. Rick had no comedy rhythm. No sense of sound. But a nicer, more hardworking guy you couldn't find. At a poker table full of drunk and stoned comedians, he was indispensable. His call, "Pot's right," kept many a stalled hand moving along. He was funny, too, when he was being himself and not trying. Rick hung around a long time, eventually working for the Toronto Blue Jays. I admired his goodness and his hustle. He was the only other amateur at that time who'd come out on regular nights just to watch.

My first sort of friend as a Monday nighter was a guy named Sean. He was a strange looking fellow. Tall, with an almost perfectly circular head, pop eyes, thick lips and a bit of a lisp which kept small amounts of saliva permanently in view. If he'd had a sense of how he appeared onstage, he might have been able to play his jokes away from it, something I eventually did successfully. The idea is that if you're handsome you talk about how ugly you are, and if you're ugly you talk about how many women you've had. Sean had this opening joke that went as follows: *It was a pretty rough week for me. You see, I'm dead. Yeah, I died three weeks ago so nothing much is going on. Although my insurance has gone up.* Somewhere in there, I see now, is a good joke. Perhaps even two. But he never got laugh one with it. It was too close. When he said he was dead, they believed him. Sean was a good guy, and his life seemed very sad. After a few months, he was gone from our stage.

In October of 1980, my father came to town and saw me perform at a little club on Queen Street. I was getting a percentage of the door, which seems ridiculous now. I think I made $25 for the whole week.

That night, the audience consisted of the other two comedians on the bill, the bartender/waiter, the owner, the owner's dog, and my father, who was the only paying customer. Dad was great that night. He laughed at everything. He didn't seem discouraged about my choice of profession at all. He was so impressed by one of the other comics that he asked after him for years. I believe his name was Kim Haberman, and he was funny. I had never seen him before that night, and I never saw or heard of him again.

That sort of ending happened a lot. For a year, two years, someone would be there, and then one day they wouldn't be there, and they'd never be there again. Sometimes that happened with jokes as well. You would do a joke for a while, a long time (I have jokes in my act now – a couple – that are fifteen years old), and then one day for some reason, coming to that place in your act where you always did this particular joke, you don't do it. And you never do it again. Then, two years later, let's say, someone says to you, "Hey man, remember that great joke you used to do about such and such? How come you never do that anymore?" And you are shocked because you haven't ever thought about that joke since you dropped it. And your act has grown in its absence, so of course there's no place for it now.

Frank Minogue was at Yuks when I started. A regular nighter, although I don't think he ever headlined. His opening joke remains one of the best and most instructive I've ever heard. *I ran into an old girlfriend the other day. I didn't recognize her till she bounced off the windshield. I got out of the car to see if she was ok, and she was ready to kill me. It's a good thing she was paralyzed.* That joke was so important for me. There are so many lessons in it. It was the first thing out of Frank's mouth after he was introduced. So many comedians start by saying "How are ya?" "How you guys' doin'?" and other forms of small talk, get-to-know-you bullshit. I always say: Start with a *joke*. The sooner you convince them you're funny, the sooner they believe it, and that makes your job so much easier. And the joke has everything. Simplicity, logic, one-line setup to joke A and a one-line setup to the tag. In perfect rhythm and easily visualized. And it answers that age-old question. Can paralysis be funny? And it can be done!

Frank had some fine material and a sick sense of humour. Something else I learned from him. Be true to your warp. If you really find a certain kind of thing funny, then that's what you should put on stage. Frank had a joke, *I had some real fun this past Hallowe'en. I invited a bunch of blind girls over and told them they'd be bobbing for apples.* Frank did all his jokes completely deadpan, not speaking slowly or quickly, which lessened the impact of how really warped some of them were. I never got to know Frank at all. I don't recall even saying hello to him. By the time I was doing regular nights, he had left the scene. But I learned a lot watching him. Or, you might say, I *took* a lot from him. He went back to his square job, telling someone I knew that comedy was only a hobby. Some of us considered our square jobs as only hobbies, which sometimes presented problems.

The security job at ManuLife lasted three months and then I was called into the boss's office and fired. Not a real surprise. But it was scary. I had to find another job quickly. Amazingly, I did. An employment agency I went to fixed me up an interview to be a messenger at Richardson Securities (now Richardson Greenshields). I was hired. Obviously they didn't know me very well. I reported on Monday morning to find that I was no longer a messenger. A job had opened up suddenly in the cage and I was the only applicant the previous week who had any university. So I got promoted before my first day. My salary was $1000 a month. Seemed like a lot.

I knew precisely nothing about the stock market, a knowledge I proudly retain to this day, but the work was mostly sitting at a desk reading stock sales off microfiche and finding and balancing discrepancies. It was a pretty easy and friendly atmosphere. After two months, I was sent to a seminar run by an evangelical South African stock trader named David Morgan. He wasn't religious. He just spoke in the lofty tones of the charismatic preacher. He ran us through some exercises that were probably ahead of their time and tried to light a fire under everyone's ass. He told us how, at age 20, with a wife and child to support, he had bluffed his way into a $300 a month job with Richardson in Johannesburg. Now, thirteen years later, he was almost a partner and was the new boss of the Toronto office, sent to turn the place around.

Mr. Morgan promoted me to Daily Box Count clerk, and one of my responsibilities was to do the bi-annual audits of all Richardsons held in the bank vaults. You had to go down into the very bowels of some bank and hand-count the securities. A more mind-numbing, hand-cramping day you could not imagine. I stayed at Richardson's long enough to do it three times. It was the middle of the second full audit that I began to realize fully that my future did not lie in this kind of a business.

But I stayed on. Tried to, anyway. 1980 passed into 1981 and I continued to go to Yuks every night, staying out way too late most nights, and sometimes not making it in to work. But the job held. I had a couple of not bad sets in a row in the early spring of '81 and Howie set up a third Monday where Mark would view the set. The promotion I wanted most was the one Mark would give me. I wore a special outfit for that set. Something my mother had purchased. Blue dress pants, a powder blue turtleneck, and over that, a white and blue striped dress shirt. My friend Steve saw me walk in and said I looked like a fag at winter formal. I thought I looked terrific. I was mistaken. I went on with great confidence and died an awful death. Outside afterward, Mark said I still wasn't ready. Then he started touching my outfit and clucking his tongue. "You don't know how to dress, either," he said sadly, to him this being a most grievous fault. I had no idea about much of anything still, but I was watching.

I started hanging out with Simon Rakoff and Howard Nemetz in the summer of 1981. Howard had a basement apartment near U of T, and he and Simon were becoming a formidable writing team. They were a perfect match. Simon was quick and explosive. He could let go on a riff and just leave you breathless with laughter at his inventiveness. He was a great host because he was so fast. He was bombing one night before a small crowd and he said, "You're a remarkable audience. Really, you defy physics. You're sparse, yet dense." Another night he had a heckler who had been successful against a couple of other comics and was feeling his oats. Simon did a joke that got nothing and the guy yelled out, "Don't quit your day job!" To which Simon replied, with virtually no pause, "Hope you can *find one.*" Howard was quiet and meticulous. He wanted every word he said to count. He had great relationship material. *The difference between loving someone and being*

IN love is subtle, but it's there. When you're in love, you phone her at ten a.m. and say things like, 'Hi. Heard you got up today...' When you love someone you have conversations like, "Oh yeah? Well fuck YOU!" He was also a great fixer. If there was a problem with a bit, he could always figure out what it was. Years later when we were both ensconced in Los Angeles he happened to see me do a set at the Improv. I had a joke I'd been working at for three months or more. I was sure it was funny, but I couldn't get the crowd to agree. It came from the fact that my father would never let us have a dog. It occurred to me one night that the only way we would ever have gotten a dog was if Dad had gone blind. I would tell the story of wanting a dog so badly and my father telling me to pray for a miracle. So I prayed, and that Christmas, Dad went blind. I thought that was the punchline. Howard said no, the punchline was the next line, which didn't even exist. "Say 'Dad went blind', and *then* say 'So we had to get a dog'." From then on, the joke just murdered. Still does. Thanks, Howard.

After work, I'd head over to Howard's and we'd smoke hash until it was time to go to the club. In the back room of his place, Howard had a giant box filled to the brim with rolling paper packets. His brother had figured out what would be a lifetime supply and they were now in Howard's possession. Drugs were an integral part of my life, starting in university, but I reached a peak in Toronto. Everybody got high. Inside the club, outside the club, in doorways, in cars in the parking lot, on the far back stairwell of the building. Legend had it that one comedian got so stoned that he got in his car, pulled out of the parking lot, drove half a block and ran into the back of a police car that was stopped at a red light. The cop walked back and tapped on the window and the guy rolled it down and said, "Geez you got here fast." We used marijuana and hash to relax, to expand our minds, to write weird material we thought was hilarious that never seemed to work, to watch movies, or just to heighten whatever horseshit experience we were currently living through. The real reason it was hard to go into work some mornings was I always had a pot hangover. But I kept the job. By the skin of my teeth.

And I kept trying to perform any place that would have me. There were a lot of venues in the early eighties in Toronto. You could do a set at Giggles, at Inn On the Park, Cafe Soho, Yuk Yuks, and others. Some comedians, one or two in particular, were always opening new rooms. Little rooms. One-nighters at restaurants that specialized in dessert and paid nothing, or in some dive bomber bar way north of town. "You take the subway to the end of the line, a bus to the end of that line, and then a cab to the gig." Larry Horowitz said one guy was so intent on finding new places, he would see a place and say, "Oh look, a crude structure of some sort. Perhaps they'd be interested in doing comedy on Tuesday nights. I'll go in and ask." Within a few years, Mark Breslin had put most of the major competitors out of business. He would simply forbid any Yuks act from playing anywhere that he didn't control. Yuks had the name and the power to give you a living, if they chose. Show your loyalty and you got gigs. Defy the emperor, and starve.

One of the most important aspects of being successful in Toronto then was learning the game. It was something a lot of guys missed. You had to know the rules and work within them, even though they changed a lot and were often arbitrary, dishonest and stupid. It took a long time to figure out all of it. Sometimes I'm not sure I ever did.

Politics aside, the real problem was being funny. My early material was almost all terrible, and building time was so difficult. Both time onstage getting your licks in and time in terms of how long you could stay up there. A good new bit will push out an old one, so you don't gain any time. Lou Dinos spent the whole first year of his career perfecting the same seven minutes, doing them over and over and over. Originality is almost impossible at the start, too, since I was influenced by everyone I saw, not to mention all the George Carlin and Richard Pryor albums I'd worn out listening to and the thousands of Johnny Carson shows I'd watched.

The first bit I wrote that gave me any consistency was a piece called the VD Record Offer. *Hear your favourite stars sing about their personal experiences with venereal disease. That's right. In this big new two-record set, called BURNING LOVE, you get them all. Gordon Lightfoot sings 'That's What You Get For Lovin' Me', along with the Guess Who classic, 'Clap For The Wolfman'.* I even made a black cardboard album cover with BURNING LOVE on it in white tape. Visual aids seemed very important then. I remember walking by a store on Yonge Street one day and seeing a sign that read, BUCKSKIN – $1.00 A FOOT. I knew another store near my apartment that sold giant comical feet so I purchased a pair and then went back to the buckskin store and asked to buy one square foot of the material. The guy thought I was insane and refused to sell me a single foot. So I found some other brownish material I could pass off as buckskin and wrapped one of the fake feet with it. I took it onstage, hidden and said I saw a sign offering buckskin at a dollar a foot, and never being one who could refuse a bargain I had gone in and bought a foot. Whereupon I produced the giant foot wrapped in faux buckskin. I actually thought this would be hilarious. Three audiences in a row disagreed completely and the great foot idea, fall '81, went straight into the garbage. I told this story to another comedian recently and when I was done, she said, "You smoked a lot of dope in those days, right?" *Right.*

I had taken a dance and movement class in university and owned a really comfortable pair of black ballet shoes and a pair of black tights. One night I wore the tights onstage under my dress pants. I complained of having been bitten to death by mosquitoes during the day and began to scratch my leg, bring my pant up higher each time. When the audience realized that black socks don't go that high they weren't entertained in the least. And again I thought this would just kill. But I kept on trying to find the key.

I wrote a joke that made me laugh one night walking home. A rare experience, to laugh out loud at something you thought up yourself. I imagined a guy on trial for murder, and he was pleading no contest. *"Your honour, ahh, I'm gonna plead no contest, right? Cause, like, I had a gun, right? And like, he didn't. So it was like, no contest."* I wrote about my dad being a lawyer. Someone told me I resembled the character 'Wojo' on the show Barney Miller, so I started doing an impression of him. I learned that placing *fuck* or *fuckin'* in exactly the right place in a joke can make a mediocre joke a killer. I wrote a play-the-field joke. *My mother told me to play the field. "Don't just date one girl. Date a lot of girls." My father also had advice in this area. "Play the field," he said. "Don't just fuck one girl. Fuck a lotta girls." Even my grandfather weighed in. "Play the field," he advised. "Don't just fuck women."* Actually I'm sorry I never got a chance to *meet my great grandfather. He was a sheep farmer in Australia.*

That joke was important because it became my closer. My big finish. Writing a bit that you can close with is an all too infrequent thing. You don't even realize you have something that can close until you get it up there and discover that nothing else you've got can follow it. It doesn't have to be your best joke. It just has to get your best laugh.

I once asked Steve Shuster what he thought his best piece was. Steve came from deep-rooted comedy. His dad was Frank Shuster of Wayne and Shuster, and his sister was Rosie Shuster from Saturday Night Live – The Funny Years. Steve said his best piece was his joke about new material. It was an eye-opener. It was the last bit I would have chosen. But I didn't know very much about comedy then. I still don't know as much as Steve does. He usually did the bit in the middle of his show. He would say, *I've got some new material I'd like to try. A lot of people have been coming up to me and saying 'Steve, DO SOME NEW MATERIAL.'* Then he'd pull a piece of paper out of his jacket pocket and look at it. *So this is brand new stuff. I haven't had a chance to learn it yet.* (Reading) *Have you ever noticed on 'The Partridge Family' how Laurie never practices?* (Look out at the audience, who are stone-silent.) *Something newer. Okay, I thought that was a good area for humour. Oh, here's one, and how about those boat people. We helped them out, now they have nice boats.* (Good laugh.) *All right, and the kids today. They're really out there, aren't they? Those scuzz-brained pus-heads!* (Puts paper back in pocket.) *I guess that one's more of a comment, really.*

Steve had a lot of problems. He would spend part of every year at a fat farm, and part of it in a mental hospital. He was schizophrenic, though never violent. He heard voices. You could be talking to him and he'd just check out of the conversation for a few moments, and then return, as though he'd never been gone. He also smoked a shitload of dope. This occasionally led to some strange stage episodes. He was performing in a bar on the night of the second Ali-Spinks fight in 1978 or '79, and Steve was a monster fight fan. He had to go on just as the fight started, and the torture was such that the stage was across from a small anteroom with a bar. There was a TV over the door that faced into the room and away from Steve. So he was doing his act with the fight going on and he could see the faces of the people watching it, which drove him crazy. At one point, the crowd watching the fight let out a cheer, and Steve couldn't take it anymore. He said, "Ladies and gentlemen, please. A moment of silence for our war dead," and he left the stage to watch a minute or two of the fight.

Fat, stoned, and schizoid, he was by far the best comedy writer of our generation. Simon once said he'd put Steve's best fifteen minutes up against anybody's. I would put his best half hour against anybody's. He could sing. He was a wonderful guitar player. He wrote incredibly funny songs. And his jokes were just sublime. Forgive me for listing some here, but this is comedy writing at its zenith.

Are there any Sagittarians in the audience tonight? Yeah? I HATE YOUR GUTS!!

Which came first, chicken salad or egg salad?

Star Search is the only show I've ever seen where the Rolling Stones could lose to Quarterflash.

You know a sport I really like? Kickboxing. The sport that combines the art of boxing.........with kicking.

People tell me I should do more topical material, but I haven't seen the news yet this year because that's when 'Rhoda' is on. Actually I haven't seen the news yet this year cause that's when 'The Odd Couple' is on. Oh, I guess that's too much like that 'Rhoda' joke. I should split those two up.

Steve could make comedians laugh, which is no mean feat. When he was on, we'd all slip into the back of the room to watch. One night we were all in there because he said he had a new song. He sang,

I can say fuck in my act, in Canada,
I draw the line at cuntface, I won't say shit or damn....

Saying 'cunt' onstage was usually death. Even the really dirty acts never said it. Steve's act was as clean as they come. I'm not sure I'd ever even heard him swear on stage up till that point. By putting it in a song, it didn't seem as bad somehow. We laughed like little kids. Then late in the set, Steve was finishing up and he said, *"I actually wrote a new piece today, and I meant to open the show with it, but I forgot. So if you don't mind, I'll close with it.* He then sang a full length number entitled 'You Should Always Open With A Song'. Again, we all reeled. He finished the song, and said, *Thank you very much. I'm sorry I said 'cuntface'. G'night.*

And there were some perfect moments when Steve would come up and suggest something for a bit I did, or even better, compliment something I'd written. His stamp of approval was Tiffany. You could live off it for a long time.

The other stamp I got was Mike MacDonald's. One night in late '81 or early '82 we were chatting at the bar of the Yuks restaurant, and he started to tell me a joke. "Did you hear they let Mark David

Chapman out of the nuthouse?" he asked. "Really?" I said. "Yeah, and he immediately tried to kill Ringo Starr." I don't know what got into me, but I said, "No, that's wrong. He immediately attacked the Lennon Sisters." Mike laughed out loud, and suddenly regarded me in a way he hadn't before. Soon after that, I began to be invited to his nightly riff and dope sessions with his crew. There were four others. Simon Rakoff, Howard Nemetz, Lawrence Morgenstern, and Ron Vaudry. Soon after that, I got promoted to regular nights. It wasn't a momentous occasion, as I recall. It had taken so long, the goal finally reached was anti-climactic. But it happened. I started working Tuesdays, Wednesdays, Thursdays, and Sundays. It would be another year before I got weekends.

There was something else, too. Mark had started a booking agency and there were a few one-nighters on the regular schedule now. And, soon after I was promoted, they started sending me out on the road.

All jobs in comedy lead to other jobs. All shows go into a place in your brain that notes similarities and differences, filing the unusual and strange. That night in Ottawa where I was heckled by a table of eight older men who spoke no English at all. The night they threw pennies at me, one of which grazed my forehead and left a small scar. The night — or nights — I lost my temper because it wasn't going well and blamed them. The two or three times I was so frustrated I called a woman heckler a cunt. And the why. WHY is he funny and I'm not? WHY can't I handle hecklers as well as he does? You can learn a great deal from watching, but stand-up, like surgery and oral sex, can only be mastered with practical experience. It's not how good or bad the shows are, either. It's the number of shows. After two hundred shows, you know five times as much as you did after one hundred shows. It's logarithmic.

EARLY GIGS

LONDON WAS an early job. The old Richmond Hotel across from the train station, if it's still there. I did it the first time with Lou Dinos. Lou was a remarkable comedy success story. He wasn't naturally funny. Dark-faced and curly-haired, he was neither bad looking nor handsome, neither jerky nor smooth. He just worked like a dog at the job. He could take a joke that had three lines till the punchline and he'd find a way to get a laugh on each line. His stage persona was a dumb but likable guy. Offstage, he was actually dumber. A very rare thing. Usually, guys who play dumb onstage – Stan Laurel, Tom Smothers – are sharp as tacks offstage. Not Lou. Someone once said of him, "Lou is very street smart, but only on his street." I learned a great deal from Lou, mostly because I never found him that funny, so I started studying what he did. The comedians who made me laugh were harder to decipher in terms of technique because I was too busy laughing.

I'm Greek. And Greek people are famous for two things. Restaurants. And Hamburgers. And hamburger is a Greek word. Ham, means grease. And Burger........more grease.

I was going to be a psychic, but I couldn't see any future in it.

Lou never wasted a word. That was something I took to heart and heavily influenced my later style. He would distill the joke down to its essence and then wring every conceivable chuckle from it. He worked slow, too. He made them wait.

London was a tough gig. As cities go, they simply don't get more tight-assed than London, Ontario. It would be easier to get laughs doing crucifixion jokes in front of the College of Cardinals. So I bombed in London. For years. Lou, that weekend, mostly killed. But who cared? I was only two years along and I had acquired a used overcoat that was too big (I thought it made me look taller) and I sported a Parisian beret. And I was staying in a hotel. So what if I looked like a complete idiot and the hotel was a dump? I couldn't tell the difference. Stupidity and naivete are so crystal clear in retrospect.

After the second show on Saturday, I headed back to my room and ordered some food in. I smoked half a joint, put on the late movie as the food arrived and settled into what was sure to be a wonderful, greasy late evening. The phone rang. It was Lou.

"Hey man, let's go out somewhere."

"No," I said. "I just got some food and I think I'll stay in."

"You sure?" He sounded shocked. *(You're the opening act. You do what I tell you)*

"Yeah. I'll see you at the train tomorrow."

"Okay." He didn't really sound that convinced.

Again I settled down with my lasagna and within a minute or two, there was a knock at the door. It was Lou. He had his coat on.

"C'mon, man. Let's go."

"Lou, I don't want to go out, okay? I don't *want* to." Again he seemed taken aback. Finally he spoke.

"Can I ask you something?"

"Sure."

"Are you gay?"

So we went out. One a.m. Saturday night, downtown London. Early spring 1982. Of course, and I knew this, nothing was open. We walked at least two miles up the main drag until we found a coffee shop that was open until three. We got there after two, stayed till they closed. I wanted to get a cab back, there being a couple waiting outside, but Lou wanted to walk back. Fucker. My lovely meal was a gluey, gelatinous mess when I returned. I was 21 years old and I wasn't even that sure, but I knew it wouldn't do to have Lou thinking I was gay.

Another early one-nighter was Charlie Chan's restaurant in St. Catharines. They had a big banquet room downstairs where we did our three-person shows. Host, middle, headliner, and a joke contest. By the fall of 1982, I was a host so I usually opened the show. It was run by a petite, fierce-eyed Chinese spearpoint of a woman named Angie. In her heavily accented English, she harped constantly about the show and our performances.

"Don't say the F-word, OK? Guy last week, Vaudry, he say the F-word all night! F-word this, F-word that. My customers, they don't like that. They more sophisticated, OK? You be good tonight, right Jan Wing? OK? You be funny, right? Not like last time, OK? I know you a funny guy, but no F-word, OK? No F-word tonight."

Some guys would bargain with her.

"Can I say one F-word, Angie. Just one?"

"No! You always say you only say one, then you say it all night, whole show!"

"Oh, come on. *Once?*"

"No."

"Fuck."

"There, you said it. Now do a good show with no F-word, OK?"

What was ironic was that the joke contest — where the host and headliner would invite audience members, excuse me, extremely *sophisticated* St. Catharinites and Wellandonians to get up and tell a joke, the best joke winning free tickets to a future show — was an orgy of smut. These tender people, so pure they couldn't stomach the dreaded F-word, would get up and tell nigger jokes, Paki jokes, graphic ass-fucking and come-shot blowjob jokes without turning a hair. But Angie stood firm for as long as the gig lasted. No F-word.

We didn't realize it at the time (who ever does?), but Angie was helping us. Working razor clean is a great asset, and puts you in the path of the really good-paying jobs. Cruise ships and sports banquets, and corporate dates of all kinds. One of the best corporate acts in the country did a company dinner gig for a large corporation in Edmonton once upon a time, and the next morning he got a call from the agent who booked the gig.

"Andrew," she began, "Did you swear at the corporate last night?"

"No," said Andrew. "You told me they wanted it squeaky clean."

"You didn't swear at *all?*"

"No."

"Did you do anything a bit off-colour or too risque?"

"No. I told you."

"Did you call someone a cunt?"

"She *was* a fucking cunt!"

ONE OF the last times I did Angie's room was in the summer of 1985. Lou was headlining and since neither he nor I had a car, we were going with David Merry, a magician. All the magicians had cars. On the way down to St. Catharines, Lou wanted to sit shotgun, putting me in the cramped back seat, half full of David's crazy equipment. Lou promised I could ride up front on the way home. When we got to the parking lot after the show I opened the passenger door and held the seat back so Lou could get in. He looked at me sadly, but he didn't move.

"Go ahead, Lou," I said. He didn't move, but gestured for me to get into the back. I brought up his promise on the way down that I would have the front seat going home. He smiled a little and put his hand on my shoulder.

"John," he said, "Who's the headliner?" So Lou rode up front both ways. And do I remember this insult simply because I'm a petty little half-Neapolitan prick? Well, ok, partly. No less than two lessons were taught that night. One was the omniscient power of the headliner, one I used many times afterward on unsuspecting young Turks, and two was that I simply *had* to get my own car.

The car story reminds me of an early gig of Norm MacDonald's. It was a four-man job in Sudbury and one of the guys, the driver, brought his girlfriend. So up front were the driver, who was also the headliner, and his girlfriend. In the back were the host, the middle act, and Norm, the lowly opener. We already knew what a great comedian Norm was going to be, but he was not fully formed yet. His writing was what was most amazing. Whole routines, word-perfect from first performance, came out of him in great draughts. Someone once said

Norm was an autistic savant, but without the savant part. Which wasn't true. He was a savant when it came to being funny. Once the audience clued in to his quirky style he had it made. But on this night he was just the opening act on a Sudbury bar one-nighter. The car they went in was a four door, but Norm had to sit in the "backseat middle" up and back. And it wasn't some pussy stay overnight gig either. They drove up to Sudbury, did the job and drove home. Two nights later, at Yuk Yuks Uptown, Norm went up to do a 20-minute set. The whole set consisted of one routine. It was called, of course, "Backseat Middle" and it was so funny we were killing ourselves, as was the audience. Norm had written the whole thing on the drive back from Sudbury, a five- to six-hour haul. The headliner, who drove all the way, told me later that Norm hadn't uttered a single word during the trip home.

Larry Horowitz taught me a lot over those first few years, and we did a lot of my first gigs together. Larry drove a beat-up blue Camaro from the seventies back then, a really cool car. And they simply didn't come any nicer than Larry. Of all the guys, he was probably the only one who made his living at stand-up who never seemed jealous, never seemed like he was competing with anyone, never wanted to put you down to make himself more important. Never. And talking comedy was something he did about as well as anyone. Larry knew every trick, every technique, every style. He talked a lot about sound. How it must be varied. Even something as simple as the voice going up on the setup, and down on the punchline, was essential. Don't let them know what's coming next. One of the biggest laughs I ever laughed was the night I saw Larry say, *"Did you hear? Morris the Cat died. Yeah."* This was done in a high tone, as though he were a neighbour calling the news across fence and yard, and then, in a *sotto voce* growl, he continued, *"I did it. I hated that fucking cat."* No pause between the sentences either. Two as one. It still makes me laugh a little, just imagining the way he performed it. Anything weird you could do with your voice was an asset. Everything that had ever happened to you was fodder. A comedian starts out like most novelists, I suppose. You want to write about stuff outside of you, things you see or read. But gradually you are drawn into yourself, into who you really are, and then the real material begins to flow. Larry showed me that more than anyone.

He would try new bits out on my rank beginner's ears. One I remember was his comment on the amazing disposableness of everything in our society. *"Yes, it's the new Drive'N'Flush. Don't be the last one on your block..."* Larry also taught me how to dress up a bit. How to layer a long routine so that by the time you get to the middle of it, there are several funny things going on at once. He was a master at that discipline. He also talked to the audience as if it were just one person, and they were having a chat. This sounds easy, but it's not. It isn't just thinking "Okay, they're only one person." It's a convivial style, an intimate, I-don't-tell-everyone-this-but-I'll-tell-you sort of thing, and it takes literally years to get it right, so it's naturally you. You never got the sense Larry was *performing* at all. He was just talking about things and you were laughing at them.

Larry was truly a comedic anomaly. He was a happy person, or at least he put on a great show of it. He was fearless, too. When challenged onstage by a particularly abusive heckler, he would occasionally invite the guy to fight. Totally serious, he would say come on outside and I'll kick the living shit out of you. I saw it a couple of times, and I found it scary, because when Larry got that look he was a scary guy. And it always worked too. The guy always backed down.

One night a drunk came up to Larry after a show to tell him a joke. He'd spent a good deal of the show heckling Larry and wanted to say hi. This was, and is, a very common thing. The guy who spent his whole night trying to fuck up your show is the first in line to fuck up your after-show. Some guy tried it with Mike MacDonald in Detroit one night and took a beating that grew more and more savage as the years went by. I don't know if Mike has ever played Detroit again. So the guy came up to Larry and said, "Man, you are really funny. I got a joke for you. What's the difference between a Jew and a canoe?"

"A canoe won't smash your fat fucking face in," was Larry's witty reply. He was quick. One night someone called him a fag and Larry said, "I hate fags. I just fuck'em to hurt'em." He even seemed to say it in a nice way.

Lastly, Larry was honest. Not cruelly so, as Simon Rakoff or Mike could be. (Or the way I often am now). Larry just never seemed to lie. He used to park his car across the street from Yuks in an old CBC lot. One night he was having a little trouble unlocking it and a passing cop noticed. Thinking he was trying to break into the car, the cop came over and asked what he was doing. Larry said that the car was old and the lock sometimes froze up and you couldn't get it open. The cop asked him for I.D., which Larry produced. Then the cop told him to empty his pockets on the hood. Larry reached into his right pants pocket and realized he was suddenly in big trouble. He had a quarter ounce bag of pot in his pocket, freshly purchased. Instead of trying to get everything else out and leave the bag in, Larry said, "Officer, I've got a small bag of marijuana here in my pocket," as he placed the contents on his car. The cop was surprised and picked up the bag. "Marijuana, eh?" "Yes, sir." The cop opened the bag and sniffed. "No," he said. "I don't think so. I think it's oregano." "No!" Larry insisted. "It's pot!" At which point his brain finally intervened and shut his big mouth. The cop opened the bag and scattered the contents to the wind. "No," he said. "You got ripped off. You have a good night now."

ANOTHER EARLY road job was the King Edward Hotel in Guelph. Larry always said that *Guelph* was the sound people made while vomiting. I did the show with Lawrence Morgenstern. Just me opening and him closing. I was supposed to do 30 minutes, and he was going to do 45. Did I have 30 minutes? No. I didn't. I had maybe 10 decent minutes, another five to eight half-decent minutes and if the audience was totally on my side I might be able to stretch it to 23, perhaps even 24 minutes. I'd been hosting a little by then and I figured I could open with six to 10 minutes of just chatting with the crowd. Easy, right? Do a few hosting tricks. Play Find-The-Asshole. My confidence might have fooled some, but it didn't fool the guy running the gig. He must have seen me blanch when I realized that the crowd was mostly college kids and they were mostly drunk and really loud. The guy said to me just before we started, "Look, if it's not going well, don't worry, cut it short."

Armed with permission, I did 12 minutes. How I managed to stay on that long still amazes me. I got *no* laughs. My banter off the top was roundly booed. My jokes were insulted. Every time I tried to pause someone would yell something. I might have been able to handle one guy, but the whole crowd seemed to be out to fuck my timing. I have never been so thoroughly flustered. It might have been the only time I ever failed to finish my time on a one-nighter as well. But the guy *said* I could. And he paid me with no complaint. And I was never booked back in Guelph again. Lawrence went up after me to a crowd now drunker than when we'd started, and three times more hostile because I'd sucked, and he did an hour. A *killer* hour. And it was a clinic, let me tell you. The definitive *How To Perform Stand-up In Bars* lecture. He did his act a little bit faster than usual, eliminating any and all long pauses and most of the short ones as well. The only pauses were for laughs. (When Simon Rakoff was bombing, he would sometimes say, *"Let me just explain that one of the reasons I like to put pauses in at the end of my jokes is to give you folks an opportunity to laugh. But I think I'll just string'em all together from now on."*) Lawrence spoke louder, too. His voice had more authority. No subtle or nuanced voice tricks that night. He just set the volume on ten and plowed through it. Not one loud heckle or screamed interruption, and there were many, stopped or fazed him in the least. By the end they were almost attentive, and they went crazy with applause when he finished. Consummate pro that he was, Lawrence never mentioned my piece-of-shit show on the way home.

Watching him that night was one of the most important lessons for me. In the two and a half years it took me to go from rank amateur to regular host with occasional road job, I attended at least 650 comedy shows, and performed fewer than 100. But seeing Lawrence that night was one of the last pieces of the puzzle. All the veterans that I tried to pal around with, and an irritating presence I must have been, kept telling me, keep writing, keep doing shows, stick with it. Ralph Benmergui used to say, "Do what has to be done. Sell the furniture, turn off the phone, go to your parents and borrow money, being sure to insist that it's just a loan that you'll never pay back."

After the show, we'd go to Fran's Restaurant at College and Yonge. Larry said it was the best place to go when you were stoned, because it had pictures of the food in the menu. So you could just point and say, "I'll have *THAT*." One night there Briane Nasimok joined us. Briane was an occasional host at Yuks. He rarely did road gigs and obviously had a better way of making a living than we did, but he was a good host and a funny guy. A wide-shouldered, sharp-eyed guy with a bowl of jet black hair and a slightly scraggly beard, he looked like a Mongolian monk. *"I'm half-Jewish and half-Eskimo,"* he would say on stage. *"When I was eight days old the rabbi used an ICE PICK!"* Briane could be gruff and intimidating, but he had a lot to say. That night he said, "Some night, you'll bomb, and then you'll know."

"Hell," I replied. "I bomb every night. So what's to know?" It got a better laugh than any I had managed onstage that night.

"No," Briane said. "You'll bomb, and on the way home you'll realize, *'Fuck* them. I'm a lot funnier than they thought.' And *then* you'll be a comic."

I don't remember what night I bombed that convinced me. There were so many. But Briane was absolutely right. First you develop material, then you begin to build time onstage, to understand timing and sound and listening. Then you begin to shape the material to fit your personality. Then you begin to develop a personality, and the last piece of this jigsaw is an attitude that brings it all together. The attitude Lawrence had that night in Guelph.

There was a sense of school, I suppose. An 'Island Of Misfit Toys' sort of thing. We were young, only a very few even in their thirties, and we had never felt we belonged anywhere else. We came from religious backgrounds, mostly Jewish and Catholic, but we were not religious. We were sports fanatics who had never been successful in participation. We were television addicts. Virtually every one of us drank, smoked, and used drugs. We lived in small, dark, under-furnished apartments. For the most part, we were unmarried. We had tempers and psychological problems. We did not like to share. We had prodigious memories for facts large and small, particularly small. Many had lived nomadic lives. We loved the Beatles, Monty Python, Saturday Night Live, David Letterman. Very few grew up in poverty. We were resolutely middle-class. We had few close friends and talked a lot about people we hated. We were incredibly insecure, champions of low self-esteem. We didn't just like attention, we lusted after it, chased it until we were breathless. We lived onstage. Offstage, we waited. We stayed up all night and slept in all day. Instead of laughing we would say, "That's funny." We had no idea where our next meal was coming from. We were only as good as our next show.

NAME DROPPING

THIS CHAPTER will be short, and I don't write it simply to name-drop, but more to give some kind of an idea of what the talent pool was like in Toronto when I was there. Yuk Yuks alone, from 1980 to 1985/86, boasted a collection of performers and writers that has few real rivals. Howie Mandel will start us off. The undisputed King. First comic to come out of Yuks and make it in L.A. Howie's bio says he went up at the Comedy Store on a dare in 1979 and the rest was history. First of all, you can't get onstage at the Comedy Store merely on a dare. And secondly, by then Howie was one hell of a comedian. Ralph Benmergui went on to become the host of Midday on CBC, had his own late night show called, oddly enough, Late Night with Ralph Benmergui, and later an afternoon talk show called Benmergui Live. Ralph was an actor and a stand-up when I met him and he gave both of them up to go back to school, graduating from Ryerson, hooking on with CBC and rising like a meteor. I've always liked Ralph, probably because his ego is almost as big as mine. And we don't care who knows it. We even dated the same girl. At different times, of course. She was too smart to marry either one of us.

Lawrence Morgenstern became the most sought-after comedy writer in Canada, head-writing Ralph's late-night show, and now the head writer of Open Mike With Mike Bullard. Mike Bullard went on to star in Open Mike With Mike Bullard, the most successful late-night talk show in the history of Canadian TV. His brother, Pat Bullard, or as we called him, 'the cute one', hosted his own nationally syndicated afternoon talk show in New York. Hosted Love Connection in L.A. Wrote for Roseanne, Grace Under Fire, and Dharma & Greg, to name only a few. Steve Fromstein, who was given the nickname Stevie Ray Fromstein by none other than me, did a couple of Tonight Shows and became a sitcom writer/producer in Los Angeles, most recently on Two Guys And A Girl.

Kenny Robinson went from being the dirtiest act in the country to the most savagely political act in the country, as well as the producer of many live comedy shows and the star of his own show on the Comedy Network. The late, great Paul K. Willis and Anton Leo became writer/producers of radio comedy, mostly for CBC. Anton has now branched out into television.

Howard Busgang and Mark Blutman went to L.A. and eventually became senior producers on the show Boy Meets World. Howard is also the head writer for all the Montreal Festival gala shows each year.

Katie Ford became a screenwriter and wrote the Sandra Bullock movie, Miss Congeniality. Chas Lawther became a very successful character actor, and his old partner, Suzette Couture, wrote the Jesus mini-series for CBS in 1999. Norm MacDonald starred on Saturday Night Live and had a sitcom and a movie that failed. Bruce McCulloch, who was a great stand-up comic, formed a little sketch troupe called the Kids In The Hall. Rick Green, of the four-man group, The Frantics, hooked up with Steve Smith as one of the creative forces behind the Red Green Show, perhaps the most successful Canadian comedy series ever.

Howard Nemetz became a successful sitcom writer in L.A. So did Jeff Rothpan and Shawn Thompson. Al Rae, the Al of Al & George, became a radio comedy writer/performer in Winnipeg, of all places, and has now begun to produce TV as well. Maurice LaMarche, a master impressionist, is the voice of many a Nickleodeon cartoon character. Steve Pulver co-owns one of the largest advertising firms in Canada. Simon Rakoff is an independent filmmaker. He was the smartest of all of us. He married a rich woman. Brian Hartt is the head writer/producer of the Fox show Mad TV. Chris Finn wrote for Mad TV, and for several years was a writer on This Hour Has 22 Minutes. Alan Watt became a best-selling novelist. Jeremy Hotz was a co-star of The Newsroom, one of the most critically acclaimed shows CBC ever did, as well as co-starring in Speed 2. Mike MacDonald is still one of the best live acts on this continent, or any other.

Now I know I'm leaving out some people. let's see now....oh yes, Harland Williams, and that impressionist guy who became a movie star, Jim Carrey.

NOW OF the 25 or so people I mentioned, 26 if you include me (And I do, Andrew Clark, I do), only Mike MacDonald, Kenny Robinson, Howie Mandel, Jeremy Hotz, and I still do stand-up comedy for a living. I was doing an audition set for the Montreal Comedy Festival at the Improv a couple of months ago and I ran into Mario Joyner, a comedian who's initial success was hosting MTV's Half-Hour Comedy Hour. He was auditioning for Montreal as well. We were talking and I said, "You know, the guys who inspired us to do this, George Carlin and Bill Cosby, Alan King, Jackie Mason, Franklin Ajaye, Gary Mule Deer, they're all still doing stand-up. Nowadays though, if you've been in L.A. 10 years and you're still doing stand-up for a living, you're a loser." "Mmm hmm," replied Mario. "That's what I am." We laughed. Then we killed and got the festival. Fuck 'em.

The goals were incremental. Get funny. Then get noticed. Then regular nights, then weekends. Then the road. Then (breathe deeply) headline the club, get your name on the marquee you couldn't see from the street unless you bent double to tie your shoes. Then get funnier. Then even funnier than that. Then get noticed again by exactly the right person and then, well, that goal was rarely spoken out loud. It was too far away and bad for the digestion to imagine it could ever happen.

GETTING SERIOUS: 1982/83

Richardsons fired me in the early spring of 1982. I had been there for almost 18 months. David Morgan called me in and said I would have to make a decision about whether I wanted to work for him or be a comic. To aid me in making that momentous decision, he canned my ass. As always, being fired never surprised me. The surprising thing was how long I stayed there. It turned out I was employed long enough to get unemployment insurance for a year, and the stipend wasn't too far off what my starting salary had been. $480 every two weeks. I also saw a way to augment that income.

The regular hosts were now Simon Rakoff, Howard Nemetz, and Ron Vaudry. There were nine hosting spots each week and they were the only paying spots on the show, except for the headliner, of course. The locals worked for nothing. For years. The hosting fee was $25 a show, and the regulars wanted more. They wanted Mark to at least double the fee. So they struck. They left Yuk Yuks with no hosts for all of maybe a day. A couple of comedians, including me, went to Mark, seeing this little action as an opportunity to get further inside the Yuks machine, and offered their services as hosts. I was immediately promoted to host and began to get regular spots on weeknights.

I liked Simon and Howard a lot, and enjoyed their company and what passed for friendship in our little club. I didn't like Ron very much, and, strangely enough, he didn't seem to care for me, either. I knew about the strike when it was being planned because I smoked dope every day with these guys. I also knew that, if I didn't act decisively, this opportunity might never come again. This is not an excuse, or an *apologia* on why I had to fuck my friends, but some instinct told me I had to go this way.

So I became a regular host. Not that I was very good at it. It was a special discipline. You had to be able to screw around with the crowd. You had to be funny off the cuff. You had to be quick and decisive. You had to know how to break your act up into little host-sized pieces. You were responsible for the show. In the beginning, I had my troubles.

Hecklers were always a major distraction. Learning how you deal with them was a long process. There were, of course, many stock lines that were used by all. *Why don't you go home, put your face in dough and make asshole cookies? I was just going to do my impression of an asshole, but he beat me to it. Hey man, I've only got five minutes up here to be funny; you've got all fuckin' night. Do I come down to where you work and kick the burgers off the grill? It's hard to believe that out of eight million sperm, you were the fastest. Man, don't be bringing up mothers. I've never even met your mother. The lineup was much too long.* Etcetera.

Some guys had their own lines. Pat Bullard used to say, "*You know, you should probably be quiet or else people will think you have a big mouth. Although, considering your sexual preference, I suppose it comes in pretty handy.*" That was always one of my favourites. Mike MacDonald never used heckler lines. He told me once that you had to deal directly with what the heckler said. Just talk to the guy, and what's funny will be there. He was right. You had to walk the tightrope, too. You couldn't turn on someone after a mild first heckle and call them a cocksucker (in so many words). You had to be judicious, understanding the mood. There were guys who would brutally assault a heckler verbally, shutting him up, and then go back to the guy later, provoking him to heckle again, and assault him *again*. But they were rare.

The hardest thing to understand about being heckled is the time factor. Up on stage, the mind works at breakneck speed. And the action is slowed down. So things that happen slowly seem to rush, and things that happen quickly are dramatically slow. Eventually I learned to almost relax my brain in those situations, knowing the right line would be there. If you needed more time, you could repeat what the heckler said. This also served as a setup for anyone who might not have heard what he said. One night in Austin I was heckled before I even said a word. I stepped onstage and before I even got to the mike, some guy yelled out, "Nice tie!" He got a laugh. I looked down at my tie, as if to see what was wrong with it *(extra time)* and said, "You think so?, I don't know. I like it. I wore this tie on the Tonight Show." Then I lifted my head and stared at the guy. "What'd *you* wear on the Tonight Show, asshole?" The crowd was all mine from that moment on.

An appearance on the Tonight Show illustrates well the idea of slow and fast. On my third or fourth set there, I was flashed the one-minute sign. It was literally a cardboard sign with *1 Min.* written on it. It was placed to the left of the camera where I could see it. I glanced at it for a moment and my brain started screaming at me. *Get your eyes away from the sign! Everyone can see you looking at the sign! You're going to lose*

your focus! STOP looking at the damn sign, you moron! Focus! Focus! Focus!
And that night I watched the set, intending to be embarrassed at how long I'd stared at the stupid one-minute sign. I watched the set, taping it, and was pleased with it. Then I remembered that I wanted to see that moment, so I replayed the tape. I had looked at the sign for less than a second. It took four viewings to see where I'd flicked my eyes over to it and then back. In that nanosecond, my brain had unloaded four complete sentences.

Nowadays, when I speak to amateur comedians before a Monday night show at Yuks, as I am occasionally asked to do, I always ask them this question. If a guy heckles you and he gets a big laugh, what does that mean? They answer everything from, "You gotta put him down hard." to, "Geez, I don't know." No one had ever gotten it right. The answer is, if a heckler gets a laugh, it means *extra time* to figure out what you're going to say in response. You can time his laugh and drop your line right on top. But only if you're relaxed. If it tenses you up, you'll rush and look like an idiot. Been there, done that.

Becoming a host changed my path. I got to do more shows, which paid immediate dividends. Within a few months I was relaxed with the audience and getting stronger reactions. My material got a little sharper, a little more pointed. And then there was that videotape I saw.

Jeff Silverman was (and is) a bear of a man, with a quick smile and a very simple corporate side. He was the real money guy; the bottom-line guy. He also hosted the weekly poker game at his lovely apartment at Sherbourne and Wellesely. I got to know him a little better in the summer of 1982 when he asked me to wallpaper the washrooms at the club for $100. I think it took me a week. He worked the sound board occasionally and he saw me host one night and said I was getting a lot better. An early aficionado of videotaping, he asked if I wanted to videotape my set some night. I said fine. I'd never seen myself perform until one night I came into the club early and Jeff called me to the sound board. He had taped me the previous night and set it up so I could watch myself right there, using headphones so no one else would hear. The result stunned me. Onstage, I was doing an impression of my college friend, John Regan.

It wasn't funny or in any way enjoyable to watch and realized that my whole attitude and style I had stolen from John. It didn't matter that no one at Yuk Yuks knew who he was. I wasn't being myself at all up there. It was shattering. And a big step.

John was an Irishman from Rochester, New York. He had the ability to walk into a room and take it over. People were drawn to his twinkling humour and devastating wit. I was both attracted to him and very jealous, since he would often be taking the focus away from me. My first year at college I spent an incredible amount of time with John, laughing and lapping up his philosophy. He played the guitar and sang on weekends at the Dominion House tavern and at the Sunday Coffeehouse at the Assumption Chapel. I learned how to play the guitar and tried to sing because I wanted to be more like John. Another friend from college, Gar Knutsen, now a Liberal member of Parliament for Elgin-St Thomas, said to me once, and I quote, "If you intend to play the guitar and sing in front of people, you had better be really funny." And I was getting along in that vein, but it was all a fake. I was just doing John. Once free from people who knew him, I had appropriated his personality.

Life was pretty good in the summer and fall of 1982. I was doing sets, I was financially stable, I was getting better all the time, and I was seeing great comedians every week. Mark had started to book a lot of American acts into Yuk Yuks and I saw Ritch Schydner, who had reams of good material. He liked to come into a club and ask what the all-time record was for the length of a headliner's set, and then break it. The waitresses hated him because on Friday and Saturday night late shows he would regularly do an hour and a half. One night he did an hour and forty-seven minutes, which I believe is still the record. I saw Gabe Kaplan, Billy Braver, Carol Leifer, who was Ritch Schydner's wife at the time. She was so good, it was scary. A pure jokewriter. Bob Dubac, a comic magician. Bob Nelson, a real artist. He had a bit called "Watching fireworks". He would hold a balloon up to the mike and scratch it with his fingernails, the sound being exactly like fireworks. After a few moments he would stop and say "Oooooh." Then a few more scratches, and he'd say "Aaaaaaah", followed by a more scratches, slowly stopping, the way microwave popcorn peters out, and then, when it stopped, he would say, "That's *it?* That was shit." Sandra Bernhard worked Yuks in that period too, but I didn't care for her. She was all attitude. Mark even booked the ancient Leonard Barr, a cadaverous old man who stood stock still and told old jokes like, "I was walking down the street and I saw a woman who had her left breast hanging out. I said, 'Lady, your breast is hanging out.' And she said, 'Oh my God, I left my baby on the bus'." Leonard was so old that he couldn't stay up late enough to headline the weekend late shows, so he'd go on early and one of the regulars would finish.

I started seeing a psychiatrist that year. In my first session I told him I didn't want to be so neurotic but I was afraid if I was cured I'd lose my comedic edge. So I wasn't exactly maturing yet. But I was beginning to see things about myself that eventually paid off.

In December of '82, on the second anniversary of John Lennon's death, an old Sarnia buddy came over and we dropped acid. It was my first time. I had been invited many times by comics to drop acid, but I didn't really trust any of them, and I had always declined. My old friend from home had done it before and I felt sure he could guide me through it if I got paranoid. He once told me that on his first acid trip he was staring at the album cover of Kansas's *Point Of Know Return,* and he'd always thought that spelling it k-n-o-w was a cute affectation, but when he was on acid, he *really* understood what they were getting at. Despite this, I still was keen to try it.

We took the tabs at noon on a perfect Toronto day. Sunny, cold, no snow or wind. At the half-hour mark, I had a raging stomach pain, which he said was normal. After roughly 20 minutes, the pain subsided, and suddenly I was so stoned I couldn't focus my eyes. We put on our jackets and went out. As we exited my building, two guys on the street called out, "Hey, look at the two guys on acid." I still wonder how they could tell. We went for a long walk up and down Yonge Street. People with animal and dragon faces passing us at what seemed like great speed. We sat outside a restaurant pointing out people and saying what animals they resembled until we were laughing ourselves silly. We went to the University of Toronto and flew around the campus for a few hours, it being deserted on a Saturday. We imagined ourselves to be totally amorphous, taking the shape of anything we brushed up against. I spent at least an hour sitting in the park at the end of Wellesely Street, my now laser-eyes taking in the traffic on the circle and the trees, all bare in the cold. But I could hear them growing. I could fucking see them growing.

Darkness came, and we headed back to my place. Suddenly my friend had a vision. "You know what we need? We need pot." I suggested that I might know where to get some. So we walked up to Sherbourne and Wellesely where Jeff Silverman lived with his girlfriend in the great apartment where I had played poker. Jeff always had some pot. I knocked on the door and Jeff was certainly surprised to see me and a guy he didn't know, but, ever the gracious host, he invited us in, sat us down in his living room, and got us something to drink. Then he said, "John, I'm amazed. In all the time I've known you, you've never just dropped in. What's the occasion?" My friend said, without missing a beat, "We're on acid and we need pot." Jeff didn't throw us out, as he probably should have. He merely dropped a few marijuana buds and seeds into an envelope, sealed it, gave it to me and ushered us out. We headed back to my apartment and smoked the envelope empty.

Now, still tripping on acid and stoned to the gills, my friend wondered what we could do. I looked at the clock and it was 7:15. "Why don't we go to the Leaf game?" I suggested. Of course. It was only three blocks away, and tickets in greys were only seven or eight dollars at the time. We strolled down Carlton Street, I hustled us a couple of greys, and we saw the Leafs get murdered by the Vancouver Canucks 7-3. They were an awful team then, and how we loved them. Two blue-suited businessmen from Vancouver sat next to us and they must have wondered, because we were screaming at everything and anything. I'm actually glad my memory doesn't hold our exact words. After the game, we went for another walk, then took the Queen streetcar to the Beaches, where my friend had an apartment. There we listened to music until around one o'clock, just waiting for the stone to dissipate. I remember going to the bathroom and not being able to find my penis because my body had no moisture left in it and my dick had inverted. The next day I had my very first hangover. Oh, to be young and stupid.

SOMETHING ELSE happened that fall that was significant. I met a girl. I had dated a bit in my first couple of years, but it wasn't easy, having little money and no prospects to speak of. My sexual encounters were few and rather completely unsatisfying. I was even starting to wonder about my ability in this area. A woman I'd dated briefly asked me along to the El Mocambo one night, to see Ralph Benmergui, who was singing in a '60's cover band called the Stingers. A bunch of us went and I happened to be sitting at a table with a feline beauty named Judy. We hit it off to some degree, though it was difficult to tell in those days. She was a theatre student at U of T. I didn't think much about it until New Year's eve at Yuks, the last New Year's I would have off for 12 years. After the big show, the club would be cleared of tables and we would all dance until the wee hours. At this party, I again encountered Judy, and this time we danced and talked and found much to like about each other. She was housesitting for someone on Yonge Street and I walked her home. She wrote her phone number and name into the book I was carrying, Public Enemy Number 1, The Alvin Karpis Story. I still have it. What I was doing bringing a book to a New Year's eve party I don't know, but I rarely went anywhere without a book in those days. They came in handy if you met someone who wanted to give you their number.

I phoned her and we started to tentatively see each other, off and on for a couple of months. Then she picked me up in her car, something I didn't own yet, and we drove to a secluded spot at U of T, where we necked a little and she informed me that she'd been seeing another guy as well as me for the past few weeks but had broken it off with him and decided to see me exclusively. Even now, I can hardly believe I beat out the other guy.

Judy was the youngest daughter of a wealthy family who lived in ritzy Forest Hill, an area of Toronto that I knew about from the jokes. Simon Rakoff also came from Forest Hill, as did a comedian named Steve Pezim. Simon called Forest Hill Collegiate "the home of the iron-clad hymen". Pezim used to say, "I had a very tough childhood. I had to ask for everything I got." Although I wasn't a churchgoer anymore, I still considered myself a Catholic and Judy was Jewish, but it didn't seem to matter in the beginning. We fell in love and that was the last piece of the puzzle for me. The confidence she gave me was immeasurable. She awakened me sexually, *found* me sexy, even. She thought I was funny and gave me excellent tips on how to improve the show. A month after we began seeing each other, I was promoted to weekends.

The first weekend I ever performed, in February of 1983, was the coming out party of Jim Carrey. Jim's manager, Leatrice Spevack, had a long-running feud with Mark Breslin, and she was always being banned from the club. Mark had no use for anyone who thought he might be screwing his comedians. One of their reconciliations finally brought Jim to the club, and he made the most of the opportunity. He was a master impressionist. His act included Sammy Davis Jr., Charles Aznavour (no kidding), Tim Curry singing "Sweet Transvestite" from The Rocky Horror Picture Show, Paul Anka, Johnny Carson, and a Bruce Dern impression that never failed to make me laugh. He closed by singing "My Way" using all the voices he'd done during the show. It was a beautifully written and perfectly performed show. He got a lot of standing ovations and encores, and so much press that Mark held him over for a second week, something that hadn't happened before and hasn't happened since. The amount of press he got was later beneficial to all of us.

Groucho Marx once wrote about seeing a slight Englishman in a vaudeville house around 1911, whose act climaxed with him spitting crackers all over his leading lady. Groucho had been impressed. The next time he saw the man was 10 years later, in his palatial home in Los Angeles. By then the little Englishman, Charlie Chaplin, was the most famous comedian in the world. I think of that story whenever I think of Jim. He went to Hollywood right after his big two weeks and, after a few false starts, he became the most famous comedian in the world. And he's still the same guy in most ways. A nice guy.

A bunch of things happened in the spring of 1983 that pushed me along the path. The first thing was moving. One night at the poker game, Larry Horowitz mentioned that he was moving out of the apartment he shared with Tony Molesworth, and Tony was looking for a roommate. They lived in a large two bedroom hallway apartment at Sherbourne and Wellesely, the same building where Jeff Silverman lived. I think Lawrence Morgenstern and Ron Vaudry all lived there too at one time. The rent would be $250 a month, a $50 increase over what I was forking out for my shithole one-room. I had also discovered that my landlady had been coming into my apartment when I wasn't around and she even accused me of smoking dope, the bitch. I approached Tony and he agreed to take me on. I was so mad at my landlady that I decided to move in secret. So on a sunny March Saturday, I packed three suitcases full of my crap and lugged them as well as my TV out the back door of the building, through the alley to Sherbourne Street and then up the long block to my new place, which, thankfully, was only on the second floor. It took four trips and was backbreaking, finger-constricting work. I made many rest stops. When it was all done, I returned to my place on Homewood, took a last look around, which didn't take more than a minute, left the key on the desktop, resisting the urge to leave a note saying *fuck you,* and took my leave. Larry had left me his big double bed, and I bought a chair and a dresser to fill out the room.

Living with Tony was a lynchpin in my education. Tall, rail-thin, with long black hair and a droopy mustache, he resembled Goofy, the Disney character. He had been working for money in show business since he was 10 years old. He was the epitome of the professional entertainer, the variety artist. He could juggle anything. He could ride a unicycle and juggle anything. He was an accomplished ventriloquist who worked with two puppets, Adam the Hippie, and Jake the Rabbit. He was a damn fine stand-up as well, and could handle a show without any props if he had to. He had a magic act and a clown act as well. I have never met anyone in my life as multi-talented as Tony.

I finally headlined the club around this time, a $500 week.

Everyone who'd been promoted off amateur night in my first or second year had already headlined, which had been very frustrating, seeing them pass me, but Mark finally agreed to put my name on the marquee. I really didn't have the requisite 45 solid minutes, but everyone headlined before they were ready. You needed the week of long shows to develop your long set anyway. One night of my week, someone timed my set at 19 minutes. Very embarrassing. The crowd wasn't laughing much and I was rushing my material. I had written a song about breaking up and having finished the lyric, I decided it was a piece of shit. The only good thing about it was the last line, which read "I hope you die a painful death before you're old and grey." So I scrapped it and wrote a new song, a very simple little thing, based on the last line. It is still a solid piece of material.

Woke up this morning, and you were gone,
I found a note, it said so long.
You said this love would last our lives,
I hope your face breaks out in hives.

I hope you die a painful death.
I hope you choke on your next breath.
You screwed me up, you done me wrong,
I hope you die before too long.

I hope you have a heart attack.
I hope your breasts get really slack.
You were my girl, but now you're not,
I hope you die, I hope you rot.

Cause I don't want to be your friend,
I only want your life to end.
You're back in town, someone else's gal.
I hope you drown in the Love Canal.

I hope you die a painful death.
I hope you choke on your next breath.
You screwed me up, you done me wrong.
I hope you die, before too long.

I hope you die before I end this song
I hope you die, I really hope you die.
Die die die die, die die die die.
Real soon.

The last chorus I used as a singalong, encouraging the audience to sing for anyone who'd ever dumped them. Only once in the almost 20 years that I've performed the song has an audience declined to sing. Despite the black nature of the song, it was without a doubt the best thing I'd written up till that time. Steve Shuster mentioned to me that he thought it was a good song, which was high praise indeed.

The press that Jim Carrey got in February prompted the Globe and Mail to send someone out to write an article on the 'new comics' in March. I didn't know the guy was there the night he saw me, which was probably just as well. He also saw Lawrence and Simon and Howard Nemetz and Ron Vaudry, who had formed a sketch group called The Needles, while continuing to work as solo acts. He interviewed them and a few other people. I was surprised to get the call for an interview and I met the guy, John Haslett Cuff, at the diner around the corner from my apartment for a chat. Then he suggested I get out my guitar so he could take a picture of me for the article. In the empty lot across from my building I posed with the guitar, holding it upside down over my shoulder. On Easter Saturday 1983, the entertainment section of the Globe and Mail opened with a giant reproduction of that picture. I was the focus of the first part of the article, and there was a later section on The Needles as well as some other comedians. But I got the lead, and it shocked everybody, including me. My father was so proud he could have busted, although my grandparents didn't like the fact that I lived in a building where "the halls stank of urine". This was because a lot of homeless people would seek shelter in the lobby and on the stairs on the cold nights. I remember the line introducing me said, "John Wing smokes like a desperate man." John asked me about the ultimate goal and I was embarrassed to say it, but he prompted me and I admitted that it was the Tonight Show with Johnny Carson. "But let's face it," I said, "It's a pipe dream." And it was a pipe dream. Then.

One thing I was quoted as saying in the article struck me. At the very end of my section, I said that when the audience was with you and you were rolling in the laughs, it was better than sex. Something clicked when I read that. *Comedy is better than sex.* I loved talking about my girlfriend problems and my woeful sexual inadequacy onstage, but this was an idea that would bear remarkable fruit. Judy loved it and I began to see a different way of doing the show.

I was beginning to understand what I looked like by then, what impression they formed about me before I spoke, and I wrote a joke that played against that. I described myself as a stud.

It got a huge laugh, and set me down the road to writing the 'Comedy's better than sex' bit. It took at least six months to get it sharp, although I added variations over the years. It was a formula piece, and a comparison piece. Within the formula, you could do virtually the same joke in endless variations, finding which ones fit next to each other in the building of the laughs from good to great to applause. Here's one way comedy's better than sex, and now, here's another, and don't forget this third way, etc. I ended up doing the bit on television at least five times, maybe more. It became my signature bit. The first piece of real comedy I ever wrote that would always be associated with me. But I was always tinkering with it, because I was at last beginning to understand that you must never, ever be satisfied with a joke, or a routine, until it's perfect. Until all the laughs are there and they build and they're big and loud every damn night. I learned that by giggling on this setup line, I would elicit a louder response. My facial expressions began to flow naturally with the material. I now had a great opening for the act. A signature piece. And a great closing, the Breakup Song. Now all I needed was a middle.

At first there wasn't any real direction, any sense of how you put your life together. It just played out in front of you and you went with it. You did the gig, met someone who told you about another gig. You phoned the guy and booked the other gig, where you met someone else, who told you about somewhere else, etcetera. Then you started booking things well in advance, putting your year together. A tour of this province, a bunch of one-nighters in that state, and it began to add up. Your photo was now on the wall in a bunch of places. Your sense of direction improved. You took a vacation by staying home.

THE REAL ROAD: 1983/84

Tony was a hard worker, constantly going over material, and writing new bits for his many acts. What impressed me about him was that he didn't depend on Yuk Yuks for his living, as I and many others did. It was a precarious existence. If you did something wrong and they decided you were being bad, they would simply not book you at all for a few months. Luckily, that never happened to me. But I was beginning to understand the risk.

My unemployment ended in May of that year and I was a little worried about making enough to get by. Mark Breslin found me a job in a video store at Bay and Bloor, right across the street from the ManuLife centre. It was my last square job and it lasted all of one day. I came in, worked the day, and when it was done, the boss fired me. He had heard me swear in conversation with another worker, and he said he couldn't have employees who cursed during business hours. I was wondering what to do next when a new gig appeared. A comedy club had opened in Rochester, N.Y., The Outrageous Inn. Howard Busgang was one of the first comedians to work it, and I knew that I was so far down the list that I'd never get booked there unless the owners asked for me specifically. So I persuaded Howard to take me with him for the Thursday through Saturday job, and I did three free sets for the guy. They had Howard staying in a one bedroom condo where I very happily slept on the couch. The two owners of the club liked me, and promised to ask for me. One down.

Mark opened up a club in Ottawa, in the basement of the Beacon Arms hotel, a stone's throw from the capitol buildings. Howie Wagman, Mark's cousin, who had been managing the Toronto club, was dispatched to Ottawa to take over the new club. And it's still there. I began hosting shows there on a regular basis. Four and a half years later, when I left Toronto for Los Angeles, I had played Ottawa 28 times. Hosting was great because it paid more than middling, Yuk Yuks understanding that the host did more work than the middle act and was more important to the show, and because it led to headlining. Middle acts came and went. Only rarely did they move up. But hosts regularly went on to the top job.

The first thing Howie did when he arrived was set up and advertise an amateur night on Wednesdays. He knew that the club would have to produce its own talent to survive and stay current in the market. The first six months yielded a couple of guys who had promise, the best being Jeremy Hotz. He was a real hard-sell comedian at first, with his high-pitched voice and bang-bang rhythm. I said to someone once that Jeremy did his act as if he were trying to sell diamonds to a sharecropper. Jeremy was brash and cocky until one night when a new guy came in and did a set. His name was Norm MacDonald. A natural, Norm took the top spot from Jeremy right away. It was astounding how good Norm was in his first months. Jeremy, no fool, left almost immediately for Toronto. He rose through the ranks and finally changed his style to a quiet, completely deadpan delivery, which worked so well that he was number one in the country by 1988, after the top four or five guys made the great exodus to L.A.

The gig that changed it all for me was a one-nighter in Buffalo. The Tralfamadore, a jazz club in downtown Buffalo, started having a comedy night , and since Toronto was closer than New York City, they started booking a bunch of us to fill out the bills. The headliner I worked for was Jerry Dinerstein, or Jerry Diner, depending upon where you encountered him. He was supposedly the 'Robin Williams of New York' which meant he did what looked like Improv, stream of consciousness type stuff, that was actually a bunch of hack bits and a lot of tricks.

I had written the Breakup Song, and seeing as how I would now have to take the guitar everywhere, I began to write a few more musical bits. I did a Neil Young impression:

Hey, hey, my, my,
They cut off my balls when I was five.
That's why I sing so goddamn high.
Hey, hey, why, why.

MY SET went well at the Tralf, and the manager called me in to pay me my $250, which was the most I'd ever received for a one-nighter. He asked if I could stay over and open the show the next night for the singer Robert Hunter, who was the lyricist for the Grateful Dead. Two shows, he said, and they'd pay me $100. I asked why I was worth $250 for one show one night and only $100 for two the next. It was out of my mouth before I could stop it, but it worked. He said, "You know? You're right. Okay, we'll pay you $250." I agreed immediately and the next night I went out before an audience of Deadheads. They really liked my drug material best, which was hardly surprising. I really should have had more of it by then. I was smoking marijuana every day now. But never before the show. I had my pride and my professionalism. Ha Ha.

Robert did his show and he went over very well, wowing them with 'Uncle John's Band,' and 'Friend of the Devil'. He was a nice guy too. Between shows he produced a couple of powerful joints and we got high. (I said I never got high before the show, but between shows was all right). I went out for the second show zapped and it wasn't more than a couple of minutes before I realized that they hadn't turned the crowd. It was the same 400 screaming deadheads who'd heard my act two hours before. Without a leg to stand on, since I had no other material, I began to take audience requests, which worked out fine. I would call for requests, then find a name in the cacophony of shouts and play a song by that person. Somewhere around the 20 minute mark I decided to play 'Good Lovin' by the Rascals, figuring an up-tempo number would get them going. To my shock they went mildly berserk at this choice, screaming, cheering and singing along. I finished the set and said goodnight, but was *called back* for an encore. My first encore. Robert told me later that 'Good Lovin' was a concert staple of the Dead, which was why they went crazy when I played it. A lucky instinct. A good omen.

A guy who ran the bar at the Tralf gave me his card and said he knew someone who had a bunch of work in Florida. Following up on this tip, I secured a month's work for November of 1983. I could hardly believe it. I would work a week at Giggles in Tampa, one week

ON THE WAY UP: *Hosting was great because it paid more than middling… Middle acts came and went. Only rarely did they move up. But hosts regularly went on to the top job.*

at Sassy's in Jacksonville, and two weeks at the Sarasota Comedy Club in Sarasota. The first week would be for $300 U.S., and the remaining three would be for $400. My plane ticket, on Eastern Airlines, cost $285 Canadian. I would cross customs at the airport and say I was going to Florida for a month's vacation. If I was judicious with my finances, I could conceivably come home with a thousand American dollars.

I worked sporadically through the summer and fall of '83, making my rent and enough to buy pot and some new clothes for my Florida trip. It was one of the happiest times. I would work the club on a Saturday night, hosting both shows, kicking ass and taking names, then head home with a small pizza or a panzerotti, watch TV in my room until I fell asleep, and be awakened by Judy. She had a key to my place now and would come in at all hours and demand sex. Being awakened by a naked, insistent woman on top of me remains a most pleasant memory.

Finally, the big day came, and I, who had always hated leaving home and been homesick on every trip I'd ever taken as a boy, boarded a plane in Toronto and flew off to the last school.

THE CLUB in Tampa was about a mile from Busch Gardens. The three-bedroom condo where we stayed was another mile or so on the other side. Arriving, I found a comedian from Michigan named Sinbad. He was six-foot-five and built like a linebacker. He had just started in comedy and was being managed by the Tampa club owner, John Cochran. There were four comedians at the condo that day. Paul Kelly and John Caponera, both from Chicago, would be there the whole week, working the show with me. Paul headlined, John middled, and I opened the show. It remains to this day the best show I've ever been on. Sinbad was staying with us for a week doing guest sets until Cochran could find him another gig. He had commandeered the third bedroom upstairs so I was relegated to the old blue couch downstairs. It wasn't so bad. It gave me control of the TV, and I could always sleep anywhere, with the exception of a moving bus.

Paul was a short, bushy-haired fellow with glasses and a thick mustache. He looked a bit like a terrier, and onstage, he acted like one, holding the mike stand tilted out toward the audience in a defiantly aggressive pose. His act was a created world, like Mike MacDonald's, but not as physical. Paul relied on long, ornately structured bits, rendered beautifully with his perfect timing. He talked about things, rather than laid out jokes. One bit I remember was about the miracle at Cana, where Jesus turned the water into wine. He would state that he assumed everyone knew the story, pause and say,

Well, we could review it. The Bible says it was Jesus' first miracle, but it was really just his first public miracle. He and Mary went to this wedding and halfway through the reception, Mary comes over and says, "Jesus! They're outta wine." Now she wasn't cursing there. She was just talking to her kid. So Mary says, "Jesus, they're outta wine. Why don't you go back in the kitchen there and do one of your little tricks?" See Jesus had been doing miracles around the house for years by then. You know, it's Sunday night and Mary's tired. She doesn't wanna do the dishes. You know, 60 Minutes is coming on and she says, "Jesus! I don't want to do the dishes!" And Jesus says, "Well verily, verily I say unto you, the dishes are already done." So Mary knew Jesus could help out at this wedding so she told him to get in there and do something about the wine shortage. But Jesus said no. You can look it up. Jesus said, "Woman you know my time has not yet come." But Mary was a Jewish mother and she just said, "You GET into that kitchen and turn that water into wine!" So Jesus went into the kitchen and he saw two men standing by a large cask of water and he told them to take it out to the reception and it would be turned into wine. And they just looked at each other and said, "Yeah, THIS guy's been here awhile." The Bible says that. It says they were skeptical. But they carried the giant cask outside and lo and behold when they got out there it had turned into wine. And all the guests who drank said it was the best wine they'd ever tasted. Stands to reason. Jesus isn't gonna turn water into wine and come out with Mad Dog 20-20.

Perhaps I remember it so well because I saw every second of Paul's nine shows that week, and he did almost an hour every time. He was topical and regional. He always opened with Florida material. I mentioned that to him one night and he grinned at me. "Always open by making fun of them," he said. "They like that." He did a bit on Ronald Reagan deciding to attack Grenada, which was a big topic at the time. The Marine barracks bombing in Lebanon was fresh in everyone's mind. All over the state, hotel and store signs said "God Bless our boys in Lebanon." Paul had Reagan stomping around the office.

Damn, I could use a victory. Jim, what's the smallest country in the world?
That would be Grenada, Mr. President.
Well, I think we can handle that. (Big Laugh)

JOHN DID a more traditional style of act, with a lot of old jokes mixed in with his versatile voice and characters. He was a very good looking guy and did a couple of pieces that were so amazing I've never seen anything like them since. One was his closer. He would say, "Ladies and gentlemen, the American Gigolo." Then Blondie's song 'Call Me' would blare out over the speakers, really loud. John would don sunglasses and do the Richard Gere shoulder-walk as he headed into a bar. He would wave to his friends and look around, ever the master of his silent domain, then pull out a soft pack of cigarettes and begin to tap the edge of it to get a cigarette to come out. He wasn't looking at the pack and the cigarettes just came flying out, one at a time, like little torpedoes. All over the stage. It was amazingly funny. Finally, John would reach into the pack and take one out, light it up and the music would abruptly stop. Then he'd tell a long story about his dick being as big as a vaulting pole. The story was humourous, but the physical piece with the cigarettes was what made it.

Another bit he did was called "School For Elvis Impersonators", in which he would be the teacher at said school, showing the men the tricks of the lucrative Elvis Impersonator trade.

My name's Randy Shelton. I've played Vegas. And I think with a little work, you too, most of you, some of you, can play Vegas too. Remember that this is just the beginner's class. Just the basics, the fundamentals. Next month, those of you who make it to intermediate Elvis will get your scarf, and your belt, and your drugs.....

I found the bit hysterical but the audience didn't always get it, so John didn't do it every night.

THE CLUB was a big one. It probably could hold 500 people in a pinch. The owner, John F., seemed like a nice guy, if a bit oily. The scene was what was so crazy. Cocaine was everywhere then. John F.

did at least a gram every night at the club. The bartenders did coke. There was a copying machine in the green room. I never saw anyone make any copies, but they cut lines on the glass all the time. The action was fast and I should have felt out of place, but I was anxious to show that I wasn't some smalltown Canadian hick, so I went with the flow. Except for doing cocaine, which I stayed away from. Not out of any righteousness, but because it scared me. Marijuana was my speed, and there was certainly plenty of that. Caponera had rented a car, so we all went out every night after the show to this bar or that bar, and then I would have to drive home because everyone else was so plastered. Once we were back at the condo, we'd break out the joints and smoke, watching late-night TV and talking comedy till the sun rose. Paul believed that you had to talk about what you believed in, what interested you and what was relevant. John thought that it should be funny, no matter what it was about. Sinbad said everything was funny, if you looked at it the right way. I still remember a night when we got back around one a.m. and Sinbad started talking about his life. He talked fast and he never stopped. I fell asleep at three and he'd been going non-stop for two hours. I awoke at five thirty, and Sinbad was still talking....

The drug use was enormous, it seemed to me. It was the first time I'd ever seen a guy smoke grass, snort coke and drink all night, and then take a Quaalude in order to sleep. I was truly an amateur next to these guys. The bartenders had a trick. They would circle around at either end of the long crescent-shaped bar, holding long matches that you buy to light fires with. The matches lit, they would pour a copious amount of whiskey straight into their mouths, then turn toward each other and spit into the flame, which would blaze up from one end to the other. It was a wonder they didn't set their hair on fire.

One afternoon late in the first week, I came into the condo to find Paul talking to the strangest looking fellow. He was about five foot ten, with a Buster brown bowl haircut that looked ridiculous around his pointed face. He wore a nondescript T-shirt and those horrible early seventies patterned golf pants only a mother could buy, along with black socks and sandals. He looked like the true village idiot. Paul introduced him as 'the best jokewriter in America'. His name was Emo Phillips. That wasn't his real name, of course. He had a peculiar high-pitched voice and he seemed nice enough, but the best jokewriter in America? Come on, Paul, be serious.

When I was eight my parents moved to Downer's Grove, Illinois, and when I was eleven, I found them.

When I was a little boy, I would always say to my father, 'Tell me a story, daddy. Tell me a story.' And he would say, 'No Emo, you know I have to get up early and look for work.' And I would say, 'Oh, come on. Tell me another one.'

I've got a new girlfriend and she's great. Last night I made love to every part of her. From the top of her head to the tag on her toe.

But he was the best jokewriter. He probably still is.

The best story about Emo was when he was starting out in Chicago. Everyone liked him, though they found him a bit weird, but he was a ghost. No one knew anything about him, except that he lived with his parents in Downer's Grove. One winter night Larry Reeb offered him a ride home, and Emo accepted. Larry and another comedian sat up front with Emo in the back seat. They got to the exit for Downer's Grove and Emo told them which way to turn. They got on a long street that seemed to just go on and on. "Where is it Emo?" Larry would ask. "Just keep going," Emo would trill from the darkness. "You'll see it." For a couple more miles Larry said nothing. Then, 'Come on, Emo. Am I even on the right road?" "Just keep going.....you'll see it. You'll see it." Finally, after what seemed like miles and miles, the road curved. Around the curve, under a streetlight, Larry saw a house and a driveway. In the yard was a snowman with three heads. Larry didn't say a word. He just pulled into the driveway. "G'night fellas," Emo crooned. Good night, Emo.

Watching Paul and John perform all week was just glorious, and I began to get a bit of a feel for the 'comedy's better' routine. Paid my $300, cash, at the end of the week, I headed for Jacksonville by bus to the next adventure.

Sassy's was probably the first video club in Florida, and maybe even one of the first in the country. TV's everywhere in the main room. Rock videos constantly playing. The comedy room was set apart, a longish rectangle with the stage at the far end. You entered through the kitchen. We stayed at the cook's house. I was actually co-headlining this job, which was astounding. The other headliner was a guy named Joe DeCaprio. A New Yorker who was older than most of the comedians I had met up to that time, Joe was also a throwback to an earlier age of comedy. He had a Catskills kind of act and was one of those guys who was always trying to make everybody laugh all the time. The trouble was, he wasn't funny at all. Always dressed like a bad radio salesman, the black hair perfectly coifed, the dress shirt and golf pants, the white belt matching the shoes, he was constantly cracking bad jokes. He had balls though. He once walked into a roomful of comics and said, "Is this funny? 'My wife had a garage sale. Now I got no place to park my car!'" Someone with more experience than I informed him that it wasn't funny. He disagreed. "I think it'll get some laughs."

Joe and I alternated the closing spot that week. Neither of us had 45 solid minutes, but we both had enough swagger and bullshit to make it look like we did. The opening act was another New Yorker named Joan St. Onge. She got the good bedroom at the cook's house, while Joe and I shared the other one. I didn't really share it, just kept my suitcase there and slept on the couch. Joe was a good enough guy to work with, but a bit creepy to share a room with.

The night I recall most was the Friday of our blissful week. I had the closing spot and the show was not particularly well attended. Joan, who really wasn't very funny, opened up poorly and Joe did his usual workmanlike set of 30 to 35. I came out to an audience that was mostly drunk and oddly spaced around the well-lit room. It was the first week they'd ever had comedy at Sassy's and the lighting guy wasn't too sharp on his stoned feet.

I went up and found a tall , blond guy, no older than I, occupying a seat right down front. Drunk as a lord, he proceeded to fuck with me for almost the entire show. Hell, he became the entire show within 10 minutes. Every time I'd try to get into a bit, he'd yell something and I'd have to respond. The bouncer didn't pay much attention to the show and so I was on my own out there. Luckily, I had some experience with unruly audience members by now and I gave the guy one hell of a time. Virtually all my good laughs were at his expense. I shot him down so many times that I got to where I was enjoying his humiliation. His friends were embarrassed and left before I was finished. He finally shut up and quit the showroom when I had about five minutes to go. I closed with my dating advice bit and came off somewhat proud of myself. I'd dealt effectively with the guy for close to 40 minutes and had gotten laughs all through the show.

I exited the stage and headed for the main room via the kitchen. I had barely entered the main room when the guy appeared from around a pillar, blocking my way. Something I had noticed about a lot of men in Florida at the time was that they all seemed to carry knives in little leather cases clipped to their belt. This guy also had a little leather case on his belt. But it was open. His hand came around from behind him and he clicked open the switch-knife, thrusting it toward my throat. I backed up a couple of quick steps and started to breathe really hard, figuring this would perhaps frighten him. As he waved the blade around my throat, I happened to look over his shoulder and I saw Joe sitting at the bar perhaps 40 feet away, transfixed, staring right at me.

"You think you're pretty fucking funny, don't you?" the guy slurred. I was too short of breath to respond, and it seemed to dawn on him that he'd really scared the shit out of me. He waved the knife one more time and put it away.

"Fucking asshole, you better watch yourself..." he managed as he walked off. I staggered, literally, to the bar, sat down a couple of seats over from Joe, and ordered a coke. Joe sidled up next to me and stage whispered, dead serious, "If he had taken one more step, I woulda been all over him." I almost laughed.

Later I informed the bouncer of what had occurred, and he said he'd keep a lookout for the guy. He wasn't kidding. The guy tried to come over and talk to Joan and me later, but the bouncer got in front of us and shooed him away. When we left, the bouncer walked us to Joan's car. As we approached the car, the guy again appeared out of nowhere, and this time the bouncer wasn't playing around. He slammed the poor bastard against the hood of Joan's vintage Mustang, took off his heavy shoe and started whaling on the guy's head with it. The sound of the sole striking the guy's skull was amazing, almost like bat hitting ball. As Joan and I watched, the bouncer beat the guy to a pulp, with Joan finally screaming for him to stop before he killed the guy. The eerie thing about it was that the bouncer never got angry or emotional. He trashed the guy within an inch of his life and when he advised us to get out of there he wasn't even breathing that hard. The guy lay in a bloody mess on the pavement when we drove away. Joan talked hysterically about the incident for a couple of hours, till we both got stoned enough to forget it. For a while.

The final two weeks of the trip were spent in Sarasota, a somnambulant community. I lived in a condo with Al April, a former salesman in his mid-forties from Jackson, Michigan. Al was the most easy-going guy in the world. He spoke so slowly that you had to train yourself not to interrupt him. Onstage he did his act as deliberately as anyone I'd ever seen. It was another lesson. He was *exactly* the same guy onstage as he was off. A rarity. He occasionally had trouble with the audience but once he got them into his rhythm, he got big laughs. It was great to follow him, too, since the crowd would lock into my faster rhythm right away.

The first week the headliner was a San Franciscan named James Wesley Jackson. A black man about Al's age, who also did his act slowly , sitting on a stool. He played a Jew's Harp to great effect, and had some wonderful jokes, although I can't for the life of me recall any of them. James was also a pussy hound, trolling for women every night. If he couldn't score at the club, he'd go out to a local disco and try his luck there. "Got to find me some pussy," he'd say after each show, although he pronounced it Puss-say, which made it a more cosmopolitan pursuit. James was a *General Hospital* addict. The only time I ever saw him get angry was when Al and I came in one afternoon, talking loud and joking with him while it was on.

"Hey, man, what'cha doin'? It's my *story,* man!"

"Sorry, James." We quieted down and he offered us hits from his giant water bong. James smoked dope from the time he got up until he went to bed, as did Al. And me, too.

The days were so long that month. There was always a reason to get up. The best reason. You had a show that night. I can't fully describe how wonderful that feeling was. I formed the habit of going for a long walk down our street in Sarasota, ending up at a small diner that had my favourite video game. I would spend the bulk of the afternoon there, eating the fantastic cheeseburgers the guy served and playing Fighter Pilot. Then back to the condo for a late afternoon bong hit or two, some TV and then the show. And I was being paid.

I even managed to have some sex while I was there, the first road sex I ever had. Al hooked me up with an older woman one night and I (wonder of wonders) picked a girl up after the show another night. By then I had used a method for some time. My "safety" pass, I called it. I would begin talking with a girl and try to subtly (yeah sure) ask for sex very early in the conversation, figuring that the ones who were interested (virtually none) would say okay, which would save a lot of small talk bullshit, and the ones who were offended (virtually all) would go away. You'd either get fucked or get home in time to watch Letterman, both of which were great. One night in Sarasota, to my shock, a woman said okay right away. You read about these things in the pages of the classier filthy magazines but you never expect it'll happen to you.

The second week in Sarasota, the headliner was a guy from Detroit named Jeff. A champion drinker, doper, and lech. He was rail thin, with sandy hair and an auburn mustache. He had some cute bits, one of which was a story told with candy bars. He played a little guitar, though he could barely sing a note. *I did a lot of drugs in the sixties,* he would say, *but now I don't care what the temperature is.* A nice enough guy, though dangerous to be around at the end of the evening. He would drink hard liquor on stage, the first guy I ever saw who did that, and he would drive drunk or stoned, or both, so you never wanted to have to depend on him for a ride.

The last night in Sarasota, Jeff was desperate, having not been laid all week. He found a woman between shows and persuaded her to stay for the second show, after which he would take her out. Going up for about 40 people, he was already somewhat drunk and determined to show this babe what he could do. In reality, he had barely 40 minutes of stuff, but that night, riding high on Manhattans, he managed to do an hour and five minutes, and clear the room. There were 40 people when he started and four when he finished. He took the girl back to the condo, asking Al to get his money for him. Al and I hung around until we got paid, and then we headed back. Smoking dope in the living room, the only light being the TV, we were startled when the girl emerged from Jeff's bedroom, fully dressed. She headed for the door, then paused and turned to us.

"Tell Jeff I said goodbye," she said. We assured her it would be done, then we laughed our heads off after she left. Apparently Jeff had been so drunk that he'd passed out either before they had sex, or very soon after.

The best story I ever heard about Jeff happened a few years later in North Carolina. He was set to get married in Detroit a couple of weeks after the gig in Charlotte, but he met a woman one night who invited him back to her place. Upon arriving there, they repaired to her bedroom upstairs and started, well, fucking. Locked in their passionate embrace, they were surprised to hear the door open downstairs. Well, perhaps Jeff was more surprised than the woman. A gruff, angry voice was heard calling her name, and she said, "It's my husband! You've got to get out of here. He's *crazy.*" Jeff wasn't even into his underwear when they heard the guy coming up the stairs. He was drunk and sure that his wife had some guy there, having seen the strange car parked outside. The woman shooed Jeff into the bathroom, naked. He prudently locked the door. Before the guy got in the room she managed to hide Jeff's clothes, but the guy wasn't fooled. Finding the bathroom door locked, he screamed that Jeff better come on out, *or he'd shoot.* This new development frightened Jeff so much that he tried the window. It was easy to open, and when the guy put a shot through the door, Jeff jumped, breaking his leg on the pavement two floors below. He managed to crawl to his car and get to a hospital, and finish the gig. (The show must....you know) He got married two weeks later in a thigh-high cast, telling his fiancé that he'd slipped on the ice coming into the club one night. North Carolina being famous for its dangerous ice patches in October.

So I came home from Florida after working 29 out of 30 nights, 37 shows total. I had $900 U.S. in my pocket, and a bunch of contact numbers for bookers all across the U.S.

I WENT BACK to Florida for the month of June 1984, where I broke my record, working 31 nights in a row. The scene had changed a bit by then. It was scarier. John Cochran's cocaine habit had cost him half the club, which was now run by a Puerto Rican coke dealer named Bruce, the single most frightening individual I've ever met. Getting paid was becoming a difficult task, but I was lucky. They knew I was a pot smoker, definitely not a cocaine guy, so they never tried to pay me in drugs. I developed a system that worked to perfection. On the two Saturdays I worked the Tampa club, I would wait until John had gone into his shuttered office to snort, then I would be at the door when he came out, asking if I could get my dough. He was usually so happy and stoned he'd get it right away. Some other guys weren't so lucky. Tim Walkoe, a Chicago comedian got knocked unconscious by Bruce when he protested that they owed him over $1000.

It's funny the guys, and their lines, that you remember. Don Gavin, a Boston comic, would say, *When was the last time you people used crayons? College, right?* Jerry Elliot, a Detroit native, who kept an old copy of the National Enquirer in a plastic slipcase because reading it was his closing. He would tell the audience it was last week's edition. Al Romero, an insult comic, the first I ever worked with, who would tell me what guys I should never play cards with. Mitchell Walters, a big genial degenerate gambler (he was one of the guys never to play cards with) who went around writing VHB on everything. VHB meant, "very hairy bush". Steve Sweeney, a south Boston boy who talked about the madness of television, comparing the daily news to "Leave it to Beaver".

Beaver lost his baseball cap? Oh my god, no! War, famine pestilence, people dying of AIDS, hey, don't bum me out! BEAVER LOST HIS BASEBALL CAP!!!

I think Lawrence Morgenstern's "Beaver" bit was the best.

First of all, who would name their kid Beaver? "Oh, we'll name him after you dear." "Mr Johnson, I'd like you to meet my son Beaver. And these are my other children, Anus, Scrotum, and Bag. Anyway, typical episode, Ward would come home, "Oh June, oh June. Where are the boys?" "Wally and the Beaver are upstairs drinking their milk." Fat lot she knows. (Beaver and Wally smoking a joint) "Hey, great shit Wally!" (Beaver looks in the mirror) "Hey, I even look like a beaver now!" Ward would call them downstairs. "Oh boys. Oh, boys. Come on down here, I want to read you some psalms." "Well, gosh dad. Wally don't wanna hear no psalms. He got Mary Ellen Rogers pregnant!" (Ward is shocked) "Wwwwwaaaallly? What's this I hear about you getting Mary Ellen Rogers pregnant? And on a school night, no less?" "Well, gosh dad. Lumpy Rutherford held her down..."

But I digress. Of course by the second time I went to Florida the guitar was a staple in my act. I had written several musical pieces, and that summer I wrote a parody of the Willie Nelson-Julio Iglesias hit, "To All The Girls I've Loved Before". I had some good lines in that one.

To all the girls who shared my life
Who turned around and told my wife...

I was doing Willie Nelson's "On The Road Again" as well. Joe Cocker attempting to sing 'Up Where We Belong', my old Neil Young. But something wasn't exactly right. The music bits were good and it was great to be able to change the pace at 35 minutes and pull out the guitar, but again, it wasn't perfect. Someone would have to tell me a joke first.

Florida in June is a fascinating place. It rained every day at four p.m. for 45 minutes. Every fucking day. It was the most constant weather I'd ever seen. There are lizards everywhere. And palmetto bugs, extra large cockroaches that don't scatter when they see the light, they just stare. And lesbians. One night me and Jerry Elliot snuck out to the parking lot to watch two lesbians make out for about a half hour. We almost missed the second show.

And there was another week in Sarasota with Al April. Al would usually head north for the summer and work the Michigan and Ohio circuit, but that June he had hunkered down in the heat and stuck it out. He came north the next year and had an interesting experience when he worked Windsor.

Leo Dufour ran Leo's Komedy Korner in Windsor, and naturally he booked a great many acts from Detroit. Leo was a comic himself and he'd known Al forever. Al was supposed to be coming in for the week one Wednesday, and he hadn't shown, which was unusual. Al was always very punctual. Leo was starting to get worried when the phone rang. It was Al.

"Leo," he began in that ridiculously slow northern Michigan way of speaking he had.

"I'm down here in your local hoosegow."

"What? What happened Al?"

"Well, the customs guys at the tunnel searched my car and found a joint that I couldn't find when I was out of pot last week."

"Do you want me to come down and bail you out?"

"No, they've offered me a place to sleep. It's an upper. But I'll need you to come to court at ten tomorrow morning. OK?"

"No problem, Al. We'll be there." So the next morning Leo and a few comics were present when Al was brought in, handcuffed on a chain with nine other guys, all of them filthy and scummy looking. Al of course, in his red golf shirt, blue dress pants that never lost their crease, and his red white and blue golf shoes (spikeless), looked truly incongruent among the rabble. When his case was called he stood and the judge, reviewing the matter, commented, "You're a bit old for this kind of thing, aren't you, Mr. April?"

"Your Honour," said Al, "I am embarrassed to tears."

"Fifty dollar fine," the judge intoned, "And don't let me see you here again."

A FEW MONTHS after I returned from Florida the second time, I was browsing through a magic shop on Yonge Street and found a magician's joke & patter book. In it I found my joke about being in bed with a woman one night, and alone the other 364 nights. The book was published in Tampa and had only just come out. What a coincidence. I worked 31 straight nights that second trip and when I got back to Toronto I was as hot as a pistol. I still had a lot to learn but I was sharp now. I had a consistency of performance. If you perform consistently, night after night, that's what you get. My material was getting better now. I was making – well, almost – a living. It had only taken four years.

All comedians want to be rock singers. All rock singers want to be actors. All actors want to be directors. Steve Shuster had a joke: "We asked Mrs. Johnson if she thought she could write a Tide commercial. She said she thought she could, but only if she could also direct."

NOTEBOOKS: 1984

READING MY notebook/journal that survives from 1983/84, I am struck by the number of legitimate song lyrics I attempted to write. Always a sucker for a sad ballad, I filled page after page with them. Bad poetry, too. Some jokes or ideas for jokes, most never used. A set list or two, difficult to decipher now, and phone numbers. Lots of phone numbers.

The set list for a Rochester show looks like this.

<u>Rochester Set</u>
    Dick Ide (crossed out)
    That's Incredible
    Whore (crossed out)
    Chinese-lawyer
    Hemorrhoid
    VD - John Houseman (John Houseman crossed out)
    Jack Barry
    Whore - Catholic
    School - Our Lady - Nuns
    Sister Addicta
    Maybe pizza joke (crossed out) Captain Tony
    Dad - Christmas

Wild Kingdom joke - maybe circumcision
Reagan - Trudeau
Taxes - Gay burglar
No Contest
Sirhan Sirhan (crossed out)
High school - St. Francis
Jock stud
Wojo - Clark - Underdog
Boxing - chess
College Bowl
Alexa - Honda - Groin
New girl - Domination - Big nose
Bodybuilder
Stomach balls - Real men - Great girl
Low standards - oral fixation
Grandparent's advice - Don't just (crossed out)
Elvis Costello
Joe Cocker
Endless phlegm
Fat out of Hell
Neil Young (circled, crossed out)
Willie Nelson
Cash for Life
Burt
Song
Beverly

I will now attempt to decode this. Dick Ide was (and might still be) a Rochester car dealer who did his own commercials. Always open with a local joke. I did an impression of Dick that I stole from John Regan, who first did it for me in 1978. Apparently, my regular opening joke at the time was a riff on the TV show, That's Incredible. I can't recall a thing about it, except to suggest that it was probably a dick joke. (I would phone my father and tell him whatever new joke I might have, and he'd invariably say, "Just another dick joke.") Chinese - Lawyer was an attempt to make something funny about my Chinese sounding surname. My father's Chinese. He's a lawyer. He launders money. I was so convinced of the humour of this one that I used it to barely titters for almost a year. Five years later, I finally wrote a good joke about my last name. Next on the list comes a hemorrhoid joke that was probably just a killer. I'll bet it was one of the big laughs of the early part of the show. I can't remember it at all. I probably should be grateful about it, too. Then we have my old standard venereal disease record offer. The John Houseman joke was a parody of the Smith Barney commercials he used to do. I would say, What's next for John Houseman. McDonald's ads? At McDonalds we make burgers the old fashioned way. We buuurrrnnnn them. I stole the idea and punch line from something Peter Cook said on the Tonight Show one night. I don't think I performed it for long. Jokes came and went. Jack Barry was the host of a game show called 'Joker's Wild'. The joke about him was a basic, what's-this-guy-like-at-home bit, something all comedians owe to Robert Klein, whose joke about the racetrack announcer Fred Capposela was the first of its kind. The joke was given to me by Howie Wagman, the owner of the Ottawa Yuk Yuks.

It was a play on Jack always saying, "Joker.......joker.......and a triple!" when the contestants would spin the wheel, or whatever it was. Switch it to the bedroom at home and Jock says, "Orgasm.......orgasm.......and a triple!" A funny, completely derivative joke that got big laughs as long as 'Joker's Wild' was on the air.

The earlier, 'whore' joke was crossed out because I was moving it to another part of the show. It seemed to fit better leading into the Catholic material. It was a joke about meeting a 15-year-old prostitute on the street one day. *Can you believe it? Fifteen years old! And there I was......broke.* Then the Catholic school stuff. All the comics, Jewish or Catholic, did stuff about their religion. All the Protestant comics suffered from a lack of religious upbringing. I think I called my church Our Lady Of The Evening, and did a bit about a nun on heroin, Sister Addicta was her name. I don't know what the Maybe Pizza joke was, and Captain Tony doesn't ring a bell either. I have a brother named Tony, but he was never a captain. They were both probably dick jokes.

Dad - Christmas was a true story about my father coming to me one Yuletide to say he had defended three men on drug charges that week.

"One of them got three years," my father said, "so he'll miss three Christmases. Another got six years, so he'll miss six Christmases. The last one got eight years, so he'll miss eight Christmases. Does that say anything to you, son?"

"Yeah, Dad. If I ever get busted for drugs, I won't be hiring you to defend me." What my father said to me was all true. My comment, thought of a few years later, was not. Looking at it now, it seems odd that Dad never considered the possibility of parole in assessing the number of Christmases missed. Closing off this mini-drug routine was a joke about dropping acid while watching Mutual Of Omaha's Wild Kingdom on TV. *And I accidentally killed my cat.......with a blowtorch. You know, I was trying to light a cigarette from across the room...etc.* That joke left the act for a short period in the middle eighties and was able to return triumphant (and funnier) in a different bit. It was always a wonderful thing to find a place for an old joke in a new bit. Something you had once discarded was given new life. Or is that being too sappy about material?

Maybe circumcision meant that I might do the bit or I might not. It would depend on how the show was going. Sometimes when the show wasn't going as you'd hoped, you'd have to switch to some new topic, some new ideas. *Here's another one you may not care for...* The key was not to give up on the audience too early. Stick with your stuff. It's your fault they're not laughing, anyway. The truly 'bad' audience is largely a myth. There are some bar audiences, and maybe the Christmas week crowd at a strip club, who aren't good, but mostly, 99 percent of the time, when a comedian bombs, he's to blame. But back to circumcision. I'd seen a doctor on Phil Donahue who said that circumcision should be the decision of the child, and the parents should wait until the boy is twelve or thirteen. I thought that would make an interesting conversation. *Son, you've got a choice. You can go to the doctor, and have him cut the end of your dick off. Or not. Gosh, Dad. I may have to think about this one.* Just another dick joke. A good one, too.

The next entry says Reagan - Trudeau, and I don't remember the joke. I can't imagine what I thought was funny about either guy. The next joke, about taxes, also draws a blank. The gay burglar joke I stole from a conversation I had with someone. They blurted that out and I used it in the show. Maybe that wasn't exactly stealing. As long as whoever said it wasn't a comic. *Have you heard about the gay burglar? He breaks in and redecorates.* I had a much better joke (one I wrote myself) that I rarely used. It was about my grandmother being robbed. *Yeah, a cat burglar broke in; stole all her yarn.* I still use that on rare occasions. My no contest joke had survived a couple of years now, and I see that it belonged more in the drug bit, but structure and thematic purpose weren't my strong suits then. Sirhan Sirhan was on television asking the California Parole Board to release him, and he said, "If Robert Kennedy were alive today, he would want me to be free." Maybe I was putting Sirhan into the no contest joke. I'll bet that's what I was doing. Taking an older joke and finding a topical context for it. Paula Poundstone did the best joke on Sirhan's comment during that parole application. *Man, what a tough break. The ONE guy who could have helped you, and you shot him!*

And off to high school, St. Francis In The Bag or some such thing. Probably a dick joke. Then an early attempt to establish what a great athlete/cocksman I was. As my stage character developed more fully, I was able to use that idea to much better advantage. Wojo - Clark - Underdog were impressions. Wojo, from Barney Miller, was suggested to me. Someone said I looked just like the actor on the show who played him. The impression was all of two words. *Uh, Barn?* The laugh was as much for the brevity as the authenticity. Putting my glasses back on, (I wore horn-rim, coke-bottle thick glasses then) I would do Clark Kent, another two-word epic. *Uh, Lois?*

Then Underdog, which I can't recall. Probably a two-word dick joke.

I don't know what I said about boxing. But the theme was still high school as I went into a diatribe about the yearbook photos of the chess team, *six acne-infested mongoloids,* the academic award winners, *same six fuckin' acne-infested mongoloids,* and the Reach For The Top team, *four acne-infested mongoloids, with the other two in the background, playing chess.* I am embarrassed to say that the joke was a staple in my act for over two years. I was learning about how to write, but I wasn't there yet. Alexa is my sister's name, and I don't know what joke I did about her. The Honda joke was something I saw a guy do at Yuk Yuks in 1980. He was a week-night regular whose name escapes me now. Probably Dick Something. He didn't last. By the time I made it to regular nights, he was long gone. He used to say, *I can still remember the car I lost my virginity in...a 1980 Honda.* It popped into my head one night when I was hosting somewhere and I did it to a big laugh. Since he wasn't around, I appropriated it for my own act. Of course, each year, the Honda would be upgraded. It was a 1983 Honda when I started doing it. A nice car. I stopped doing it in 1989. Not that it wasn't still working. I just forgot to do it one night and never did it again. That would happen more frequently than you'd imagine. Someone would come up and say, "Hey man, why don't you do that joke about such and such anymore?" And you would have no reason. It just slipped out of the rotation one day and was forgotten. The two jokes it was separating fused into each other so well that you didn't need it anymore.

And then a bunch of dating jokes. My specialty in those days. I've probably written more than a hundred of them over the years. There are ten on the list. Groin - new girl - Domination - Big nose -

Bodybuilder - Stomach balls - Real men - great girl - low standards - oral fixation. There are only two of these I think I can reproduce. The others can be guessed at. (Dick jokes?) New girl was probably a basic, I've-got-a-new-girlfriend joke. *She's a good Catholic girl, named after a saint...Bernard.* It might be that one, although I think I wrote that a couple of years later. Domination is probably about the same girl. Big nose was a joke I had for a long time. *Her nose was huge. It was bigger than a part of my body I call 'Bob'. I took her to the movies and some guy used her nose as an armrest. Asshole. Knocked my arm right off without even asking.* Stomach balls intrigues me no end, but other than saying it might have been two jokes, one about stomachs, the other about balls, I draw a blank. Real men was obviously about the book, Real Men Don't Eat Quiche, which was quite popular at the time. Jeff Gourlay had the best line about it. *A real man has his woman make quiche for him, and THEN he doesn't eat it.* The only other joke I think I know is the last one. *I'm not picky. I don't ask for much in a woman. All I ask for is that she's a nice person with a lot of money and an oral fixation.*

Then we have some musical bits. A short parody of Elvis Costello's 'Alison'.

Alison,
I know I look like a geek today,
Alison,
Fuck me anyway.

Embarrassing to even think of now. I didn't think I ever did that one onstage, but if it was in the set list, I must have performed it a few times. Then Joe Cocker, the title of the song being 'Endless

Phlegm'. It was a parody of his hit with Jennifer Warnes, 'Up Where We Belong', and all it consisted of was the first two or three lines of the song, followed by an apoplectic coughing jag. Hysterical. Fat Out of Hell was a joke about Meatloaf, I think. I don't think I did a song there. Then Neil Young, my old standby; the only thing I retain, slightly better written, from my very first set. Willie Nelson's 'On The Road Again' followed Neil. *And it's great to be lying on the road again...'*. Cash for life was a joke about the lottery. *The doctor told me I had six months to live, and the next day I won the Cash for Life lottery.* Burt could have been a song, but was probably a joke. Probably a dick joke. It led into the Breakup Song, now a crowd favourite. I closed with Jimi Hendrix playing the 'Beverly Hillbillies' theme song. I would turn my back to the audience and hoist the guitar behind my head. Finding the mike to centre myself, I'd do a couple of false starts and then play it at breakneck speed. A turn and a flourish with the guitar and thank you very much. You were a great audience. Tip the waitresses. Try the veal.

That was my brilliant act after three and a half years. Close to 60 jokes. About 40 minutes in length. Forty-five if they were hot. Less than 30 if I was bombing. Mostly dick jokes, with very little structure or thematic purpose to the show as a whole. The message seemed to be that I didn't get laid enough. It's humiliating to admit that the message hasn't changed all that much in the intervening 20 years. I just do it better now. The dick jokes are much classier.

The notebook could be called, 'Versions', because most of what I wrote was bad and I kept trying to improve it with rewrites. There were no less than five attempts at a song about the girl next door being a stripper. A childhood neighbour was for a brief time a stripper in Toronto, and I was inspired by any success story from the old neighbourhood. There were two versions of a Serial Killer Confesses song, never used. Three versions of the Almost Song.

You're almost everything to me,
And I could take you almost anywhere.
You're almost all I'd ever want a girl to be.
And when you're sad and blue I almost care..

I think I like it better now than I did then. I tried it maybe once or twice, but I just wasn't sure it was funny, and without supreme confidence, the audience can smell a loser. I dropped it after a couple of tries. A draft of a Dear Penthouse Forum song, never finished. Howard Nemetz had the best Penthouse Forum bit. (Reading) *'After ramming my twelve and a half inches'* (Oh God) *'into her pulsating pussy'* (NEVER *have I seen one pulsate)* *'for FOUR hours, I decided to come.'* I *decided to come. I wasn't aware that you could make that decision. My girlfriend's reading the letter and she says, 'It says here he decided to come after four hours. How come you decided after 30 seconds?'* I make QUICK *decisions, okay?* Once I saw that bit, I was no doubt inspired, but everything I thought of was just a rehash of Howard's idea, so I gave up. On a back page of the notebook, almost hidden, is an early draft of a song I did bring onstage, and one day I'm going to bring it back. As soon as we see the white smoke again.

Oh if you know the game you'll remember my name, I'm the Pope.
With one toll of a bell I can send you to hell, I'm the Pope
I can't have a wife but it's such a great life I don't care,
. Cause everyone loves me and nobody sits in my chair.

Oh, I'm the Pope, and I come from Poland,
I'm the Pope, I like to go Bowlin'....

Phone numbers, set lists, mawkish songs, funny songs, jokes, poems, and a couple of letters I thankfully never mailed. A decent notebook for a young comedian. I was only beginning to realize that where there's one joke, there's ten. And where there's one gig, there's a hundred. But you need a car.

Two guys walk into a bar. Which is really stupid because after the first guy walked into it, (smacking forehead with hand), you'd think the second guy would have seen it.

Howie Mandel circa 1982

JOKE WRITING

Mark Breslin went on trips to New York and Los Angeles every year to find new comedians for the club. You had to have something special if he was going to book you. Steven Wright he brought in when Steven had barely 30 minutes of material, but Mark's prescience was rewarded when Steven got the Tonight Show within a few months of playing our club. Steven was a revelation to many of us. He did jokes that were in many ways unlike anything we'd ever heard. He sort of wrote them backwards.

Joke writing, for the most part, involves steps. One starts with one or two logical steps on a topic and then adds the absurd step, which either sets up the joke or is the joke. After that, all the tag lines are logical extensions of the absurdity. I'll use an old joke of mine to illustrate. *I dated a smoker once. She liked to smoke during sex. Which I didn't mind, so much. It was that cold ashtray on my ass. A little disconcerting, trying to establish a rhythm of your own, and balance something at the same time.* The first step is that she smoked. Logical enough by itself, I suppose. Then I introduce the absurdity. Instead of smoking after sex, she smoked during sex. After that, it's just simple steps. Steven would start his jokes with a premise so absurd that it was funny. Once you accepted the premise, the jokes proceeded in simple and believable steps.

I was cleaning my closet the other day and I found a bathing suit I had made out of sponges. I remember I went swimming in a pool, and then I left, and no one could go swimming until I came back.

Steven's style also enabled him to string a bunch of completely unrelated jokes into a routine. My favourite was *The other day I got into an elevator with another guy. I pushed number four, and I turned to the guy and said, "Where you going?" And he said, "Phoenix." So I pushed Phoenix. The doors opened, two tumbleweeds blew on, we got out and we were in downtown Phoenix. I said to him, "You know, you're the kind of guy I'd really like to hang around with." He said, "I'm going to the desert. You wanna go?" I said, "Sure." So we hopped in his car and we drove out to the desert. He said he'd been working for 20 years on a project for the government, trying to figure out who financed the pyramids. He worked on it 20 years, they paid him an incredible amount of money, and he told them he was pretty sure it was a guy... named Eddie. We got out to his house and it was cold. He said, "I'll get a fire going." Then he took a bunch of money, stuck it under some logs, and he lit it. Then he said, "You know, I remember when the same amount of money could light two or three fires." Five hundred miles out in the desert, the phone rings. He says, "You get it." I pick up the phone and a voice says, "Steven Wright?" "Yes." "This is Mr. Haines, your student loan director from your bank. You're 62 bank payments behind, and we just received word from the institute you attended that they received none of the $17,000 we loaned you. And we'd really like to know what you did with the money." I said, "Mr. Haines, I'm not going to lie to you. I bought myself a really nice pair of boots." He said, "Don't you think that's just a little bit irresponsible?" And I said, "Not really. They were on sale."*

Steven could wring probably eight major laughs from this piece, which consists of four simple absurd jokes, none of which having anything to do with the other, and yet seamlessly put together and performed. Watching Steven was always a lesson in writing. By the time he did the Tonight Show, he had even made the last joke better. When Haines asked him what he did with the money, he said, *"Well Mr. Haines, I'm not going to lie to you. I gave the money to my friend, Jigs Casey, and he built a nuclear weapon with it. And I'd really appreciate it if you wouldn't call me anymore."* He hadn't made it better. He'd made it perfect. It got a huge laugh and an applause break on Carson.

Of course Steven could also write jokes in the classic style. One I recall was, *Last year my friend and I drove cross country. All the way we only had one tape to listen to. I...I can't remember what it was.*

That's the essence of jokewriting right there. Take them somewhere, until they're sure of where it is, and then go somewhere else at the last second. The juxtaposition of the incongruous, to use a technical phrase. Magicians do the same thing physically. You think it's one thing, but it's really something else. Jokes are done in rhythm, and when I write one that I think is good enough to try out, I can hear it as it's written. I am testing out how it's going to sound while I'm thinking of it. The one thing comedians know above everything else is what words sound like. Why 'keepsake' is funnier than 'souvenir'. Why the smoking during sex joke is made infinitely better by the ashtray being cold. The ashtray on my ass is visual, but the cold ashtray is palpable.

The rhythm is important. One - TWO! One - two - THREE! Or, my personal favourite, one - two - three - FOUR! I don't know why I like the four-count rhythm best. It's probably just my contrary nature, given the fact that the three rhythm is the most popular.

Even now, out of 10 or 15 jokes that I write, there might be one, maybe, that's really funny and will work onstage. The difference is that now I know immediately which joke that is. In 1985 I hired Simon Rakoff and Howard Nemetz for three hours at fifty dollars an hour to sit with me and shpritz jokes for my act. There were a perfect team. Simon was inspirational and could go on amazing riffs on almost any subject, while Howard was more technical, a word-perfectionist. He would shape a joke and shape a joke until it was just right. Three hours and one hundred and fifty bucks later, we had exactly one joke for the act. And I'd written it. The most expensive joke I ever wrote. *Canadians are skeptical about religion. We believe Jesus walked on water. We just figure it was probably winter.* I still use it, so I've certainly gotten my money's worth.

In the beginning, you're trying to write one funny joke. Then, as you accumulate material and shape it into some semblance of an act, you're trying to write routines. Routines often require a formula. A hook you can set the idea on, while you lay out the lines like darts on a board. I absolutely *adore* formulas. Cannot get enough of them. To me, they make the routine easy to write. Comedy's Better than Sex was such a routine. From the basic idea, I wrote at least twenty jokes. Or, to put it another way, twenty versions of the same joke. I narrowed the group down to eight or ten jokes, later going down to six or seven. Then I played around with the order, finalized that, and began to look for what I call 'dressing' jokes. Jokes that lead you into the bit and then out again. Within these I found ways to refer back to earlier jokes, ways of running gags all the way through the piece, etc. Comedy's Better, like many routines, is essentially ten ways of looking at the same thing. You put a dot on a piece of paper. That's your idea.

Then you draw a circle around the dot and you attack it from every angle in the circle. One of those angles is the key, which opens up the dot and gives you the routine. Then you perform the damn thing several hundred times and it morphs its way into a final, perfected version. The audience has the final say, and it's by their sound that you make the corrections.

Big week for me. I became a father for the first time. (Applause) Yeah, me and some waitress from Winnipeg, apparently, had a baby. (Giggling) Didn't even remember her name, but it was right there, on the subpoena. You can all probably tell from just looking at me that I'm a stud. That's why I wear glasses. Glasses are an important part of studdery. I have two looks. (Take off glasses) This is what I look like when I'm in bed with a woman, and (put glasses back on) this is what I look like the other three hundred and sixty-four days of the year. And that's why I do comedy. Because I think doing comedy is better than sex. And I know you're all saying, 'But John. We've never done comedy'. And, I can relate. I know what you're going through. But to me, comedy's better. Comedy I perform for a whole bunch of different people. Sex, I perform by myself. Comedy's better. In Comedy, you laugh at what I say. Comedy's better. I've never had a comedy audience tell me my joke wasn't big enough. 'We prefer longer, thicker jokes, John.' While I'm performing for you people, I'm not imagining a better looking audience with bigger tits. Well, okay, I am. But they don't mean a thing to me. They're a one-thought stand. In comedy, if someone yells out, 'YOU SUCK!' That's a heckle. In sex, that's a command. And I think the women will back me up on that. After the comedy show, women come up to me and they say, 'You were great.' 'Thank you. Thank you very much.' After sex, they always say, 'You're funny.' 'Thanks for coming.' Some nights I perform comedy for forty-five minutes to an hour. Comedy's better. About forty minutes better by my watch, and I think the women will back me up on that. After the comedy show I feel good! No guilt, no post-comedic depression, no subpoenas. After sex I always fell that it somehow just wasn't worth the money. And I think the men will back me up on that. Actually my neighbourhood has a lot of hookers. They all work out of this pizza place. It's a good deal, though. If you don't come in thirty minutes, it's free.

Including tags, that's fourteen jokes. And it builds. We have a running line, 'Comedy's better', that's twice used for big laughs, in both jokes the audience writing their own punchline, really. Everything I compose even now harks back to this, my first real piece of comedy writing. I had written other bits and jokes here and there that weren't bad. But this was a completely original piece (I thought) and it made me a comedic force to be reckoned with. Too bad I can't write something this good every week.

Another guy Mark booked regularly out of New York was Uncle Dirty. His real name was Bob Altman, and he'd had a very successful career in the sixties, with a couple of record albums and a bunch of TV appearances. Then he disappeared.

"I looked up one day in 1970 and I had $175,000 in the bank. I decided I wanted to see the world." Seeing the world took the better part of six years, and took his bankroll and his career. He told a great story of returning to L.A. from Australia in 1976. He was hanging out at the Comedy Store and he ran into Richard Pryor, an old pal from his New York days. Dirty was close to being destitute and Richard was the most famous comedian in the world , having done *Silver Streak* and a spate of other successful films. He was about to do the best comedy concert film of all time, *Wanted: Live In Concert*. Go ahead and watch it if you think I'm wrong. He had a huge house in Bel-Air, and he invited Dirty to come and visit him later that same night. So Dirty drove to the gated house in the fabulous neighbourhood, and was buzzed in by a guard.

"You go right on up. Mr. Richard is in the living room." Entering the palatial living room, he saw Richard sitting on his couch, naked, a giant brandy snifter full to the brim with cocaine on the coffee table in front of him, and two model-perfect naked women with their arms wrapped around him. Dirty came by his nickname honestly and he was literally drooling at the sight, when Richard looked up and saw him standing there.

"You can't stay, Dirty," Richard said, smiling. "I'm just showing you this for incentive."

Dirty's act was political and historical and long-winded, and very much of the sixties, but man did he *know* a lot about stand-up. Sitting with him was platitude central.

"I never say someone won't make it. Jimmy Walker made it, anyone can make it." He told me one night that he thought stand-up would eventually boil down to the truthful guys.

"The guys who get closest to their own bone will be the ones making it in the future." That was an excellent piece of advice. To this day, I can write a joke about anything, but the funniest things in the show are things that happened to me. I embellish the endings a lot, but everything starts in a truthful place, and most important, rings true. And that is what makes the best comedy. And again, if you don't believe me, watch the Richard Pryor concert film. The first one.

In those days I was just a joke writer, for the most part. The best one of those at that time was a guy Ronnie Shakes. He never worked

Toronto, but he was a regular on Carson and he was so pure. *I knew a guy who was so old, he knew all the words to 'Taps'.* And my all-time favourite, *I know Hell is hot. But is it humid? Cause I can take the heat...* A perfect joke and tag in fifteen words. Impressive.

Another thing I love about the job was that it was about what you could do. I couldn't do what Mike MacDonald could do. I wasn't very physical onstage. I couldn't stand on my head and drink a beer, as Dan McGovern did. I didn't do characters like Ralph Benmergui, or ventriloquism like Tony Molesworth, and I wasn't funny to look at like Jeff Gourlay. Jeff was almost a parody of a comedian. He was a big, barrel-chested man with a goofy dumb guy persona. He had some funny bits, but what was hysterical was watching him bomb. He had jokes designed to do poorly and he got his big laughs trying to explain them to the crowd. I couldn't do that either. I tried it. Hell, I tried all of them, but I could only do what was original about me. It takes a long time to see that. Uncle Dirty, among others, showed me that what I could do was be true. Be true to my warp. I tell young comedians this a lot. Be true to your warp. If you think fucking frozen corpses up the ass is funny, then talk about it. Find a way to prove to the audience that it is funny. Whatever your *real sense of humour is,* stick with it. That's what you can do.

There's a comedian in Toronto now named Mike Cliff who represents what I'm trying to say here better than anyone else. He tells the audience what he thinks is funny. If they laugh, great. If they don't, great. He's the only comedian I've ever known who is truly indifferent to whether or not they respond. He has a joke about child-molesting. Not a topic at the top of our 'Things To Write About

Today' list, but Mike talks about it. *I went to summer camp. Camp Fuck-My-Ass, it was called. The camp flag was a tear-stained pillow.* Not for the squeamish, but one of the funniest jokes I've ever heard.

But the guy who really showed us what Dirty meant was Sam Kinison. Mark booked him out of L.A. in 1984 or '85. Seeing him was the revelation. The messiah. Mark warned me that he'd booked someone who did an act I wouldn't believe, which was saying something. But I didn't believe it. I didn't believe you could do comedy the way Sam did it, and I didn't believe I could laugh that hard for that long. Sam would come out in a long coat, a beret, shirt, jeans and sneakers, and inform the audience: *You've seen a bunch of comedians tonight. You laughed. You had a good time. And the only difference between me and the comedians you've already seen is....that you may want to see them again sometime. That's right, you are going to wish to GOD, YOU NEVER SAW ME!! AAAAAAHHHHHH!!! AAAHH!! AAAAAAAHHHHHHHH!!. And you say, 'Sam, what's the problem?' The problem? (a truly maniacal laugh) What problem? I don't have a home. I don't have a car. I didn't eat yesterday. I had to borrow these clothes. I may not eat tomorrow. SHE TOOK IT ALL!!!! THAT FUCKING BITCH!! I WAS MARRIED FOR TWO FUCKING YEARS TO A BITCH FROM HELL!! But I try not to have an 'attitude' about it.*

What he brought to the comedy stage was the style of the charismatic, evangelical preacher. The quiet buildup to sudden, earthshaking power, or in Sam's case, rage. He was legitimately funny, and very intelligent. People think that his comedy was all about his nuclear-powered voice, but he was capable of brilliance in his writing. He had a bit about what a tough job being an apostle must have been. *You can't call in sick. That would never work. (Miming telephone) 'Hello, Jesus? Yeah, it's James. Listen, a bunch of us went fishing last night, and we forgot our sweaters. Yeah, so we've got the cold here, and we're not gonna be able to walk to Jerusalem with you today.......What's that? We're healed? We're healed just by the power of your word? You don't even have to be here, you just send the word and it sets us free from disease? No, I feel great. (Looking around) No, everybody's up. We'll see you then, right. No, no, no, thank you'. Okay! he didn't buy it! We're healed. Let's go!*

It was the most amazing comedy performance I'd ever seen. Afterward, Dan McGovern walked into the green room where we were all congratulating Sam, and he said, "I *quit.*" He was half-serious, too. Nobody could do what Sam could do onstage, although many have tried. Nobody had his intelligence. From that first night, I knew he'd be a star. People reacted to him only two ways. Either they laughed so hard it physically hurt when the show was over, or they walked out in the middle, angry as hell and demanding their money back. No one, *no one,* found him mediocre. And when people got pissed and stomped out, Sam would go after them. *Those of you out there who hate me, who think I'm just a degenerate bastard spewing this filth, I'd like to do something special for you. I'd like to have the list of the names of your sacred dead. The list of people who've meant the most to you in this life who've passed on....so I CAN WIPE MY ASS WITH IT!!!*

Sam tapped into what most comics have in abundance. Excess rage. Offstage he was a pussycat, sort of. He was deeply into drugs, as were virtually all of us. One night I remember stalling the audience for 40 minutes after the last local comic because Sam refused to go on until he was advanced enough money to buy an eight-ball. Rick

Grossman, long removed from performing by then, was managing the club and had strict orders not to advance Sam any dough. But it became apparent that obeying the boss was going to leave a packed house without a headliner and demanding their refunds, so Rick finally relented and Sam agreed to go on. I was onstage that night over 70 minutes. Sam did a spectacular show as well.

Sam died a few years back in a car accident on the way to a gig. The worst way any comedian can die. It is something I have always feared. It's much better to die on the way home, after the job, or, like Dick Shawn, to collapse at the end of a show. That way people can say they saw your very last show. Die on the way and all they remember is you never showed up. A bad way to go. Sam deserved better. He was a pure flame.

A comedian gets back to his hotel room around one a.m. on a Saturday night/Sunday morning, and is watching television when there's a knock on his door. Opening it, he discovers a good looking, well-built, well-dressed woman in her late thirties standing there. "Excuse me for bothering you," she says. "I saw your show tonight and I just had to meet you." "Really?" says the comedian, pleased. "Yes," she replies. "You see, my husband died about two years ago from cancer and I just haven't been the same. The truth is, I haven't laughed at all, not once, since his death. But tonight, watching you perform, my God did I laugh! I laughed so hard. You made me feel as though I'd never laughed before. And I feel so good right now. I feel as though a great weight has been lifted off me. You did that with your jokes, and I just wanted to thank you." "Well," said the comedian, "You're very welcome." "Also," said the woman, "If there's anything I can do for you. I really feel that there's something I should give back to you, what with all the help you gave me tonight. If you have any sexual fantasies you've never tried..." she trailed off as she moved closer to him, placing his hand on one of her large breasts, reaching down and fondling him as they tongue-kissed. As they broke the kiss, the comedian suddenly held up his hands and pushed her back slightly. "Wait a minute," he said. "Did you see the first show, or the second show?"

HOTEL/MOTEL

In 1985 I BOUGHT a car. My first car. It was a dark blue four door 1981 Pontiac Phoenix. I'd been dicking around with my bank, trying to get a loan, but they waffled one time too many, so I financed it with GMAC. I don't recall how much I paid for it, but it didn't matter by then. I'd been so frightened of adding another large monthly expense to the nut, but the day came when I simply couldn't do without anymore. Paying for the car also meant driving it everywhere. I began to spend a lot of nights in hotels. Almost a hundred nights in 1985, leading to my probable peak, over two hundred nights in 1987. Of course, they weren't all hotels. Some were called condos. The comedy condo. A cheap-ish two or three bedroom apartment in a complex relatively close to the club, or not. A couch that had seen better days, a TV, a table, a few chairs. Some cooking pots and utensils. Pizza phone numbers tacked to the wall. yellow pages open at pizza places. A few magazines, some of them pornographic. A giant garbage tub. Closets with two or perhaps even three wire hangers. Smells you could never identify. And the good memories come flooding back.

Some places had the same hotel for years. The Yuk Yuks in Ottawa started in the basement of the Beacon Arms Hotel, and it's still there, although I believe the hotel has changed it's name. Howard Nemetz had a joke, *Apparently Elvis stayed at the Beacon Arms once. Of course the hotel was a lot thinner then.* For some reason, I always got a corner room at the Beacon. An end-of-the-hall room. Not as big as the rooms by the elevators. The Calgary Yuk Yuks has always been at the Blackfoot Inn. The comedians' rooms are mostly on the first floor. I don't think I've even gone above the first floor more than a couple of times in seventeen years, and I've played the club at least 30 times. The Chinook Mall is a 20-minute walk and there's a dirty magazine store just down the block. You get to know where the important things are.

Then, there's Winnipeg. I've stayed at the Charterhouse, The Sheraton, The Viscount Gort, The Hotel Fort Garry, Place Louis Riel, and at least two others. The Gort was a fun place. A couple of months after I stopped using drugs, in 1994, I ran into an old friend at the Improv in Los Angeles. Geechy Guy by name. I don't know his real name, you'll just have to trust me that his name fits him like a god-damn glove. Anyway, Geech had just come back from Winnipeg, stay-ing at the Gort, and I mentioned that I would be there in three weeks. He said he'd bought some fabulous hash while he was there but, since he couldn't bring it home, he'd stashed it behind a radiator on the third floor landing of the back stairs. I'd stayed at the Gort at least three times by then, so I knew all the nooks and crannies. I wished he hadn't told me about the drugs, because I wasted a shitload of time searching every damn radiator in the place, finding nothing but dust bunnies and some warm spiders. Some other addict with a nose for these things beat me to the cache. Geech may have felt kindly toward me because I gave him a joke once that I believe he still does. We were in Toledo (Envoy Inn) and I had this joke I'd just stopped doing because I couldn't get it to work. It was a hotel joke. *I didn't have anything to read one night in the hotel room and I found this Gideon Bible in a drawer. I'd never read it, and it was fantastic! I was so impressed, I stole it. Yeah, imagine my embarrassment when I got to that page.* I told it to Geech one night because he did a bible joke, and he liked it so much he offered me money for it. I didn't want money. I told him I doubted it would work, but he could certainly try it. Geech went up and killed with it. Go figure.

In Atlantic City I stayed at what was once the Ritz, but was now converted into apartments. I worked that week with Jonathan Katz, the creator and voice of Doctor Katz, professional Therapist. Jonathan ranks up there with Emo as one of the very best pure joke-writers of our time. He wrote a joke once that swept the country. Paul Shaffer told it on letterman one night, not realizing, I'm sure, that it was Jonathan's. *I was having breakfast with my mother the other day and I committed the classic Freudian slip. I meant to say, "Please pass the sugar." and it came out, "You cunt! You ruined my childhood."*

The first time I ever saw Jon was a Letterman appearance he did in the mid-'80s. I'd never heard of him, and he didn't look like much. Bald, with a face that defines deadpan. I gave him a glance and went back to what I was doing. (Probably rolling a joint) I listened to the first couple of jokes, not really that impressive, then the third joke snapped my neck. *The other day, I took my daughter to the cheapest carnival I've ever been to. The freak show featured a bearded man.* Hey there, who's this guy?

Working with Jonathan was a lot of laughs. We went to a strip club after the show one night, and we were sitting next to each other at the bar, nursing our eight-dollar cokes, when a large-busted blonde woman came up next to Jonathan, gyrating to the music, and pushing her tits up into his face. He turned briefly and gave me a look that bespoke surprise, and then he turned to the woman.

"Excuse me," he asked. "Do you work here?"

"Of course," she replied, her voice like whipped cream.

"Oh, thank God," Jon said, and turned back to me. "For a second there," he whispered, "I thought she was coming on to me." I laughed so hard people stared at us. I was always laughing hard around Jonathan. One night he told me a joke of his that had never worked. *I had a horrible day today. This morning I stepped into what I thought was a huge pile of Shinola.* Of course, to get the joke, you had to know the phrase, 'He don't know shit from Shinola', but I couldn't believe that it didn't work. Jon offered to give me the joke on a trial basis.

"What does that mean?" I asked.

"You do it onstage tonight," he said. "If it kills, you can have it. If it bombs, I want it back." I went on to a hot crowd, tried it; it tanked completely and I gave it back to Jonathan.

Rodeway Inn, Envoy Inn, Hotel Budgetel, Motel Six(We'll leave the light on for you to scare away the roaches), Super 8 Motel, Knight's Inn, Red Roof Inn, Howard Johnson's, Relax Inn, Courtyard Inn, La Quinta Hotels, Best Western, Signature Inn (Did you hear about the illiterate guy who couldn't get a room at the Signature Inn?), Sandman Inn, and the Holiday Inn. And most of those are just in Michigan. Tthe Howard Johnson's in Grand Rapids had a great Meijers store across the street. A sort of midwest Wal-Mart. The Knight's Inns had purple velvet bedspreads. Super 8 Motels usually had the best cable TV. Motel Six wasn't really so bad after all, and the worst hotel food by a wide margin was Holiday Inn. And I can say from recent experience that, as of July 2002, that's still the case. I might mention here that the food has to be pretty goddamn bad for me to notice it.

In Halifax, we stayed at a great hotel. The Lord Nelson. Very old style. There were mail slots by the elevators on every floor. We stayed there until a couple of drunk comedians pissed down the mail slot on night, and we were moved to a lesser lodging. In Vernon, B.C. there was a hotel that had a river running through the lobby. I stayed there with Colin Campbell, who was known as Chief because he drank 'like and Indian'. One night, Colin went out and drank up a storm, as was his custom. Returning to the hotel the next morning just before seven, he was sitting on his bed, moments from passing out, when he remembered that he had a radio interview at 7:30 a.m. He called the front desk and asked for a wake-up call at seven. "But sir," the clerk said, "It's 6:58 now." To which Colin replied, "You'd best be dialing," and hung up.

You recall the great hotels because they are few and far between. Al Michaels, the ABC sports announcer, once did an article on what he needed in a hotel. One of his comments was, "A phone in the bathroom is a necessity, not a luxury." This was before the proliferation of cellphones, but I can count on one hand the number of hotels I've stayed in that had phones in the bathroom, and I'd still have enough fingers left to jerk off with. The nice hotels are the most expensive, of course. I was forced to overnight in Dallas once, between planes, and I phoned the Airport Marriott, foolishly, to find out if they had any rooms. The woman told me I could get a smoking room, *and* I would be getting at their *Super Saver* rate. How about that? The Super Saver rate was $165 a night. This may not seem like a lot, but it is merely for better soap to steal and a phone in the bathroom. *Hi, mom. Guess where I am? The Marriott in Dallas. And guess what I'm doing? I'm taking a dump! That's right, while we talk! Is that cool or what?*

In a hotel in Big Rapids, Michigan one night, I was with Eric Tunney, a Windsor boy who started doing stand-up at 15 and is one of the classier guys, to this day. In those days, Eric was probably 20 or 21, he was a champion drinker. He might have had the largest capacity for alcohol of anyone I've ever seen, and that's saying something. He came to my room one night carrying a twelve pack of long neck beers, which he proceeded to polish off, in about two hours. I had ordered a couple of pizzas and he dug into one, and finished that off. Then he went outside to the parking lot and threw the whole thing up. I wrote a joke about it that I still use as an extro for the host. *Let's hear it for whathisname! You probably don't know this about him, but he's not only a fine comedian, he's also a great magician. Last night after the show he made twelve beers disappear, and then he made them reappear again with a pizza. (Apparently there's some trick to it.)*

A similar tale occurred on the eastern tour one year. The tour was Sydney, Dartmouth, Halifax, Charlottetown, Moncton, Fredericton, and St. John over an eight or nine day period. It was the last night of the tour, and the headliner and middle act were hanging out after the show. Bill, a semi-grizzled veteran comic, and Jamie, a fresh-faced youngster out of Etobicoke or somewhere who was doing his first real road tour. Jamie was elated at finishing the tour and was buying drinks and having a grand old time. They were sitting with two women, one of whom (or possibly both) Bill was trying his best to fuck. Jamie wasn't trying to fuck anyone, not that it mattered. He was the kind of guy who could fall into a giant mudhole because he wasn't looking and come out clean sucking on a huge lollipop and getting a blowjob from a mermaid. He didn't have a care in the world. At one point, Bill ordered a second pitcher of beer for the table, and Jamie jokingly started chiding him.

"Are you sure you should have more beer, man? he laughed, patting Bill's somewhat expanded paunch. "You're getting a bit of a pot there, you know." Bill laughed and the girls laughed, and the beer came. Then Bill ordered a few more drinks, introducing the young road warrior to some different kinds of liquor. They had some jelly shots, Jamie being game for anything. The girls bowed out after a couple of hours, but Bill knew an after-hours joint, having done this tour a few times, and they had a few more there. Finally they arrived back at the hotel, where Bill had thoughtfully called ahead and had two pizzas delivered. Jamie dug into the food like a starving man, and Bill watched. They were watching TV and after a little while, Jamie suddenly didn't feel well. He raced for the bathroom and began to lose what appeared to be an endless supply of meals. While he was retching, Bill sauntered over to the bathroom door and watched.

So, you think I need to lose some *weight*? Is that it, kid? I should drop a few pounds, *right*? Go on a fucking DIET?!"

The worst so-called hotel I ever stayed in was the Hilton in Kalamazoo, Michigan. I've been in better appointed hospital rooms. Any hotel that has the TV bolted to the ceiling or the remote bolted to the night table is a piece of shit. Once, in Vancouver, I had a room like that, and I phoned down to the lobby to ask if I could change rooms.

"Is there a problem with your room, sir?" the desk clerk asked.

"Yeah," I said. "It's full of brooms."

Only once in those years did I refuse to stay at a hotel. In St. John's Newfoundland in 1987. *The world will end at midnight tonight; 12:30 in Newfoundland.* It wasn't that it was a really bad place. It just didn't have cable. The Tigers and Blue Jays were duking it out for the division that fall and I was desperate to see the games. It was the final weekend of the season and the Jays had three games in Detroit. The fellow who'd booked me picked me up at the airport and drove me to a little bed and breakfast sort of place, which was okay, except that the TV was a tiny black and white that plugged into the wall and had an antenna. I was such a sports fan and so cocky that I simply refused to stay there. I was sure there was some cheap motel nearby that had cable TV. And there was. The guy was a bit taken aback by my fanaticism about watching baseball, but I surprised a lot of people with my silly desires in those days. I was a monster Tiger fan, which didn't make me popular with the Toronto crowd, or the St. John's crowd either, for that matter. After the show on Friday I went to a bar nearby to watch the game. It was a tense one. In the middle innings, the Jays got a runner on with one out. With two strikes on the batter, the runner tried to steal second. the batter swung and missed, and Tiger catcher Matt Nokes nailed the runner at second in a classic, strike-him-out, throw-him-out play. As Matt rose to throw to second, I rose in my seat, screaming "Oooohhhh..." Unable to control myself in my happiness, I made a giant sweep of my right arm and called, "YER OUT!!" It quickly became apparent that I was the *only* Tiger fan in the place. I left immediately and watched the rest of the game in my fabulous, hard-won motel with cable.

In 1985 I worked a club in New Orleans. Well, Gretna, really. We stayed in a motel near the airport that became famous because a few years later, Jimmy Swaggart, the TV preacher, was caught fucking a prostitute there. A really ugly prostitute. You'd think, with all his dough-nations, he'd have been able to afford a better class of call girl. Jimmy Swaggart was a fine companion in those years. He was on TV late most nights in every town, and Sunday mornings you could always find him on some channel. Once I had my car, I stopped staying over on Saturday nights. It was stupid. I wasn't going to sleep after two shows until very late, and then I'd get up late and waste all of Sunday going home. No sir. If you worked with me in those days the rules were simple. You want a ride back, we're leaving Saturday after the show. I'd pack the car and check out of the hotel before going to work on Saturday, then get my money afterward and so long, city. If you're going to get laid, make sure it's on Friday. From Ottawa on one side or Toledo on the other, I'd head home, arriving around six or seven a.m. I'd phone my dad for our regular Sunday conversation. "How's business?" Then I'd smoke a joint and watch Jimmy Swaggart speak in tongues, play bad gospel songs and talk about *"Glow-ray! Glow-ray ta Gahd!"* My pockets stuffed with cash money and my apartment glowing in the early morning light, I knew I'd live forever. Or at least for another week.

The best hotel story I ever heard was New Year's gig in Saskatoon in the late '80s. New Year's gigs were generally hell. Sheer hell. They paid very well, but, as the headliner, I'd always have to go on around 11:15, so the last thirty minutes of the show were done to an audience that wasn't listening because they were screaming and playing their noisemakers. You had to work. It was the quintessential work night. But the show was never satisfying in any way.

One year Howie Wagman booked me with Kenny Robinson for an old fashioned Ottawa New Year's. I extracted a strict promise from Howie that I would open every show. Kenny and I had a run-in a few months before in Buffalo. He was hosting that week, and believed he should be headlining, so he was doing a 35 to 40 minute set between the middle act and me. Dirty, hard-hitting material that was really difficult to follow. My fault, though. I let it intimidate me. Besides wanting to prove that I couldn't follow him, Kenny had a personal animus for me, too. I was one of the first guys booked into a club in Winnipeg in 1985. The crowd had been a bit reticent that week, and I got a strong impression that they thought I was too dirty. At the end of the week, the manager asked me what I thought of him booking Ken Robinson. I said, "Man, if they thought I was too dirty, they'll run Kenny out of town on a rail." So Kenny didn't get the gig. And, it turned out, Winnipeg was his hometown. I should have kept my big mouth shut. He got even, of course, but I told Howie in no uncertain terms that I would not follow Ken in Ottawa. Let him be up there near midnight on New Year's eve. I'd be gone by then. Long gone.

I still remember the joke Kenny opened with that week. Besides being one of the dirtiest jokes I'd ever heard, it fit all the criteria for a starter. It should be really funny and tell the audience exactly what your sense of humour is. Kenny, who disdained the 'Hi, how are ya' type of greeting, would stride to the mike, pause for a brief moment, and say, *Did you ever kiss a girl whose breath was so bad you wished you'd given her a rim-job instead?* I truly admired that joke. If you were opening the show with a joke that disgusting, what the hell could they expect for the next 45 minutes? Man, did Ken Robinson have big balls. Big brass ones. They clanked when he walked. After that week, he and I became friends, and we remain so to this day.

Of course, my little plan to have him close all the shows backfired. On New Year's eve, Ken was so ill from a drug binge the night before, that he only lasted ten minutes on stage, then apologized, ran to the bathroom to puke, and then passed out. I had already done forty minutes and it was only ten after eleven. Howie pleaded with me, and there really wasn't any choice. I went up and did another 40 minutes or so through the cacophony of celebratory noise.

So, anyway, the Saskatoon story. I got a bit sidetracked there. Three comedians worked the gig. The headliner was Roger Chandler. *Took my girlfriend to the zoo the other day. Got eighty bucks for her.* Roger was an Ontario kid who started out in Vancouver because he worked every summer in B.C. as a river rafting guide. A round faced, round-bodied guy who was as nice as they come and a lot of fun to hang around with. This particular new Year's show had gone badly for Roger. he got on late and they were very drunk and mouthy and he didn't enjoy himself at all. But he got another chance to show them he was funny.

It snowed all day December 31st, and then stopped snowing around 11 p.m. In the next two or three hours the temperature dropped like a rock, finishing up at 30 below, Celsius. Arriving in the lobby for brunch the next morning, Roger and the other comics found it packed with stranded people. Every car in the parking lot was frozen, and there was only one tow truck place open new year's day and only one guy was working. He was in great demand since every hotel in town had the same problem. So there were upwards of seventy people in the lobby awaiting jump starts. Roger had a inspiration and asked the guys to wait there for him while he retrieved something from his room. He raced back upstairs, took off all his clothes and put on a Speedo bathing suit. It must have looked pretty skimpy on Roger. He grabbed a towel and headed down the back stairway. He went out the back door, and plowed his almost naked way through the snow drifts. He slipped and fell a couple of times, but he finally reached the crowded lobby. Dripping wet, snow all over him, he strode to the front desk, pounded on it and screamed, "HEY! HOW COME THE POOL'S CLOSED?"

SO YOU get to know the hotel/motel life. You can find the ice machine by its sound. You know the best rooms are by the elevators. You finally figure out that merely picking up the phone will cost you fifty cents. You appreciate the ones with a decent complement of TV channels and despise the ones without. You never really get to know the towns much. You only know the way in to the hotel, where to park, and the way back to the highway when it's over. You can become a tourist, though I never really did. In New Orleans in 1985 I went into the French Quarter once. The cab ride was so expensive I never went back. Surrounded by what would be for many a culinary paradise, I ate at McDonald's. Some years later I worked a club right in the Quarter, and stayed in an apartment right next to it. That time I was mature enough to sample and fall in love with the local cuisine. New Orleans is one of the best cities in North America. On the Thursday night of the gig, there was a poetry reading scheduled after our show. We had 60 people for our show, and there were 150 for the poetry reading. Now that's a place to live.

SHORT TAKES

<u>BRUCE</u>

His name was (and is) Bruce Bell. He was, amazingly, from Sudbury, Ontario. Not that Sudbury hasn't produced its share of artists, but believing Bruce was from there was a stretch. One could only assume he'd fled at the first opportunity. He was a tall, lean, snobbish fellow who was a cross between Clark Gable and John Barrymore. He had Gable's mustache twinkle, and Barrymore's above-it-all debauchery. He used to say, *I'm quatro-sexual. I'll do anything with anyone for a quarter.* When I first saw him, he was doing a double act with a girl named Colleen Pierce. They were, naturally, known as Bell & Pierce. They did a variety of sketch bits, the best one to my mind their French movie parody. Bruce played a jilted lover who goes to a bridge, intending to jump off and kill himself. As he prepares to leap, he notices the woman who rejected him also getting ready to kill herself. Bruce narrated the scene on tape in a Charles Boyer-style accent.

I am standing on zee bridge, ready to jump and end my life when, what's this, my lover Marie, who rejected me, is standing beside me. I look at her. She looks at me. I turn away from her. She turns away from me. I spit at her. She spits at me. I slap her. She slaps me. We kiss.

I still think it's really funny. Bruce and Colleen broke up the act early in my first year and Bruce continued solo. He was one of the only guys working at the time who did characters. He did Vince From

Sudbury, Ontario, who always introduced his hometown with his name. Vince would tell a story about screwing his girlfriend while driving his truck. He did a confession movie ending, a parody of all the B movie endings of the thirties and forties. The scene would open with Rocky bursting in on his girlfriend.

GIRLFRIEND: *Rocky?*

ROCKY: *That's right, Rocky. Mildred didn't kill Rodney, I did. yeah. I was jealous of her and of you. I couldn't get her out of the way, so I tried to get you out of the way. With you out of the way, I figured I could get to her. But you're too stupid to see trouble when it stares you in the face. Mildred saw it and tried to escape. Heh heh heh heh, too late! She bought herself a one-way ticket to the bottom of the Hudson River. Then there was only you. Funny isn't it? How the stupid dame always ends up with a belly fulla lead?*

GIRLFRIEND: *You got it all wrong, Rocky. You got it all wrong. Mildred didn't kill Rodney, I did. yeah. I was jealous of her and of you. I couldn't get her out of the way, so I tried to get you out of the way. With you out of the way, I figured I could get to her. Aw, but you're too stupid to see trouble when it stares you in the face. Mildred saw it, and tried to escape. Heh heh heh heh, too late! She bought herself a one-way ticket to the bottom of the Hudson River. Then there was only you. Aw, can't you see, you big lug, that I love ya?*

Man smashes through the door.

JOHNNY: *Both of you, up against the wall!*

ROCKY: *Johnny!*

GIRLFRIEND: *Johnny!*

JOHNNY: *That's right, Johnny. Mildred didn't kill Rodney, I did. Yeah. I was jealous of her and of you. I couldn't get her out of the way, so I tried to get you out of the way. With you out of the way, I figured I could get to her. Aw, but you're too stupid to see trouble when it stares you in the face. Mildred saw it and tried to escape. Heh heh heh heh, too late! She bought herself a one-way ticket to the bottom of the Hudson River. then there was only you. Funny isn't is, how the stupid people always end up with a belly fulla lead?*

And on and on. The first confession would be a slow, normal talking speed. Each succeeding one would be faster until Bruce was going through it so fast it was hard to understand any of it. Bruce was a great guy. A devastating yet quiet wit. He was the only guy I remember in the Yuks crowd at that time who was openly gay. Michael Boncoeur, Paul Willis' partner in *La Troupe Grotesque,* was flamboyantly gay, but he was gone by then.

Bruce wrote a play in the mid-'80s, called *The Rise And Fall Of Tony Trouble.* It was the story of a ruthless actor who attains stardom and then, through drug addiction, among other things, falls spectacularly. It reminded me a bit of *The Oscar,* one of the greatest bad movies every made. Bruce played the title role, of course, and the play enjoyed a reasonably long run at a small dinner theatre at Gerrard and Bay Street. I happened to go to the final performance, which was a doozy. The play was narrated by Max, Tony Trouble's longtime agent, who was played to perfection by a comedian/actor named Tony Mason. He was like Bruce in that they were both throwbacks to the suave, debonair leading men of the '40s.

Near the end of the play that night, there was a dressing room scene, where Tony Trouble, now a mere understudy, is in the dressing room with the leading man, who's a real prick just as Tony was when he made it. Tony admits to the man that he is twice or three times the actor Tony is. And Tony admits he's afraid of one of the scenes in the play. The suicide scene. If he's ever forced to go on, he's not sure he can pull that one off. Could the leading man possibly show him how it's done? The actor, flattered beyond measure, agrees. Explaining the meaning, he puts the prop gun against his head and pulls the trigger. Of course Tony has loaded the gun with a real bullet. When the gun fires and the man dies, Max is supposed to burst in and say, "Tony, what happened? I heard a shot!" But on this, the last night of the show, something went wrong. The cap in the prop gun failed to ignite and all that emitted from the gun was a small *click*. Somehow, and it was masterful, Bruce and the other actor maneuvered their way to doing the scene again, and again the gun was fired. And again it only clicked. By now the other actor had had enough, so when the gun didn't fire the second time, he screamed, "Something PRICKED me!", and fell dead. Bruce, brilliant as always, turned to the audience, raised an eyebrow, and said, "Poison dart." which got a big laugh. Whereupon, Max burst in and shouted, "Tony, what happened! I heard some *remarkably* bad ad-libbing!" It was a sight to behold. Even the dead guy was laughing.

I haven't seen Bruce in many years, but when I think of him, I most often recall the night he went onstage at Yuk Yuks and said, *Ladies and gentlemen, tonight I would like to try something that has never been tried before. I am going to attempt to act my way out of a paper bag.* He then stood in a large paper bag and began doing Shakespeare. A little Hamlet. Couldn't get out. A little Richard III. Couldn't get out. Then he did an impression of John Ritter from the TV show Three's Company. *Chrissy? I don't have any clean underwear. Can I use one of your pairs?* And voila, the bag exploded and he was free. There are a few guys in Toronto now who remind me of Bruce. But really, they're just pale imitations. None of them would know how to get out of the paper bag.

OPENING

Opening for rock bands was an occasional gig in the old days. It paid next to nothing, but it was sometimes a cool thing to put on your résumé. The biggest problem was that the audience was *not* there to see you. The most famous story about it concerned a young Albert Brooks, opening for Richie Havens. Albert was standing backstage, listening to the truly eerie chant of the audience, who were growling, "Richie, Richie, Richie..." The stage manager, an old black man, turned to Albert.

"Is your name Richie?" he asked.

"No," said Albert. The old man shook his head.

"They gonna *kill* you," he said.

My first big opening job was at Lulu's Roadhouse in Kitchener in 1984. The place was massive. It had the longest bar in the world, the sort of thing Canadians love to brag about. The building was once a K-Mart, I think, or some such giganto-store. It held 5,000 people. The problem was that they were spread all around the room, so it was hard to get anyone's attention. There were a million sounds, too. The pinball machines, the video games, the drink blenders, etc. Add to it at least 25 televisions on the walls and ceilings. When I was onstage, I was on every one of them. Another unnerving first.

I opened for two-hit wonder Lesley Gore (*It's My Party, Judy's Turn To Cry*), and one-hit wonder Lou Christie (*Lightning Strikes*). I arrived early and was given a dressing room. It turned out to be Miss Gore's. When she arrived, she had me booted. I guess I'm lucky she didn't have me fired. By that time all the other dressing rooms were taken, so I hung out. The next time I worked there, I opened for David Clayton Thomas, lead singer and songwriter for *Blood, Sweat & Tears*. The coolest thing about that week was that his band would be in place behind me as my show ended, and on the last two nights, they played along with The Breakup Song. I was really honoured by that.

I have opened for the Smothers Brothers, who're not only a great comedy act, but also really nice guys. I think Dick Smothers is the best straight man I've ever seen. The only straight man who comes close to him, in my opinion, is the late Dan Rowan. Dick Martin was such a loose cannon, you had to have a great straight man next to him at all times. One night, Rowan and Martin were playing a hotel gig some-where, and the show was going badly. They had been eating it for 40 minutes when Dan decided he'd had enough. He said to the audience, *Ladies and gentlemen, we're now going to take you to the Olympics.* Although Dick had no idea what Dan was doing, he immediately started doing calisthenics, figuring (correctly) that he would be the athlete in this piece. *We're going to be watching the marathon today, ladies and gentlemen,* Dan said, *and our camera crew is going to be concentrating on the race favourite, Sweden's Sven Svernstrom.* Dick began to speak in a thick Scandinavian accent. *As a matter if fact,* Dan continued, *we have a special camera and sound man in a special car that will be following and interviewing Sven all through the race. This has never been done before in a race this long. If you're ready Sven, and...THEY'RE OFF!* Dan and Dick ran off the stage, up the centre aisle of the showroom, out the door to the hallway, to the elevators and up to their rooms. *Good night. Tip your waitresses. Try the veal.*

A few years back, I started getting jobs from a fellow in San Diego who books old performer shows for really old audiences. I opened for John Raitt the first time, and the Mills Brothers the second time. Then he put me on a sort of tour of Southern California. It was me hosting (in my tux and looking good), The DeCastro Sisters, The Four Freshmen, Gloria DeHaven, and Buddy Greco. The first night, in Thousand Oaks, I had done my squeaky clean 20 off the top and was relaxing backstage when the booker came to me and said, "I need you to do another two or three minutes between Gloria and Buddy, so the crew can move Buddy's grand piano into place." I was racking my brain for something that would fit, since I had done most or all of my clean stuff. Plus, I only had a couple of minutes, and you need something that stands alone, not something that dovetails off a previous bit that you did an hour ago to people who probably don't even remember.

Lucky for me, Gloria DeHaven was going blind. An immeasurably elegant woman at least 75 years of age, it was hard for her to navigate the distance from the wings to her mark onstage. So after I introduced her, I walked back to the wings and took her by the hand and escorted her to her microphone. Once she got to the light, she wasn't an old lady anymore. She was by-God Gloria DeHaven. When she finished, I had to go out and lead her off, and by that time I'd thought of something. I went to the mike and said *You know, ladies and gentlemen, it's such a thrill to be on a show with so many musical performers. I've never been musical myself. The only musical moment of my life was when the big flood hit my hometown in 1972. Water filled up the first floor of our house. My father went out the front window on the sofa. And I accompanied him on the piano.* It killed, and the piano was successfully moved. I first heard that joke in the late '60s, on a British television show called *Joker's Wild.* It was an early, funny version of what is now *Whose Line Is It Anyway.* I heard a comic named Arthur Askey do the joke on that show, and I'd never repeated it. I just kept it with me. Almost 30 years later, it came in handy.

Working with Buddy Greco provided another scrapbook moment. We did several shows together and eventually got talking. One night we were gabbing about something and I saw an opportunity to do one of my favourite jokes for him.

"The thing is, Buddy," I said, "I don't want to achieve immortality through my work. I want to achieve it through not dying." He liked that very much, and he reacted as a comedian would.

"Oh, that's *funny.* That's very funny. Is that yours?"

"Sorry, Buddy, no. It's Woody Allen's."

"Oh that's funny. That's very funny." Later, when Buddy was onstage and I was having a cigarette at the stage door, I heard him calling me.

"Where's John? Is John back there?" Tossing my smoke, I rushed to the wings, where Buddy motioned for me to come onstage. As soon as I got out there, he said, "Tell that joke. The funny one." And he held his microphone to my face. I did the joke. I don't know what Buddy was thinking, having me do a joke about *dying* to a crowd of people who were as close to it as you can get, but I did the joke. It got a big, thudding, tumbleweed zero. After no more than a moment of silence, Buddy turned the mike back to him.

"Get off," he said. Turned his back on me and went to the other side of the stage. I shrank down to the size of a limp dick and got off. He got the big laugh. I still owe him one.

The best working-for-elderly-people story was Andy Kindler's gig at a Jewish retirement community in Florida some years ago. Andy was talking with the old fellow who hosted the show and asked how long a performance they wanted.

"I want you to keep the show from 20 minutes," the man said. "Because we're having sponge cake. And once they smell the sponge cake, *the show is over.*"

Lulu's Roadhouse must be long gone now. No doubt it's morphed back into a Wal-Mart or a Costco. Last year I played a casino in Mesquite, Nevada, and David Clayton Thomas was headlining the big showroom. Don't be a musician, son. You'll be on the road all your life.

MIKE

His name was Mike Shapiro, though not everyone knew that. He was about five foot two, maybe, of indeterminate age, though roughly close to the rest of us, somewhere in his gleeful 20s. He had a round, cherub's face, and a beatific smile, but his eyes were a bit off. They were slightly crossed, or foggy or something. It didn't matter because he always wore sunglasses, his black hair slicked up in a fifties pompadour, and the obligatory '50s street-hoodlum outfit of black leather jacket, white T-shirt, jeans rolled up at the bottom and black biker boots. The reason that few of us knew his real name was because he called himself Mike the Macho Man.

He may have been mildly retarded. That was always my impression, though he was a very nice sort of guy. A little obsessed with the '50s, but a very nice guy. He once confided to me that he thought the '50s was the greatest decade in human history.

"And you know why?" he asked me.

"No, Mike. Why?"

"Because there weren't any faggots." He was absolutely serious.

Mike was a weekend performer at Yuks. A sort of novelty act Mark would trot out for the dinner/show weekend crowd. "Here's something a little different for you," he would say as he introduced Mike. Mike didn't have any real writing ability. I think most of his jokes were stolen or written for him. On night we were all sitting around the back of the club after show, and Mike was talking about his act, which he rarely did.

"I need to hire a writer," he said. Steve Pulver, a part-time comic who was very witty, snapped back, "Herman Melville is *dead.*" It convulsed my brother Richard and me. I'm not even sure what's funny about it now, but it was a great line then. If Mike was not a writer, then he most certainly wasn't a performer, either. He did his act in the most rudimentary of styles. The punchlines twice as loud as the set-ups. That and the '50s tough guy persona, the growling hoodlum who swore and told the dirtiest jokes. The most important thing were the sunglasses. If he'd ever shown the audience his real face, they wouldn't have believed anything he did.

He would come on, go straight to the mike, and launch. None of that 'Hi! Howya doin?' bullshit for him. He couldn't do that, because all he knew was his act. He couldn't shpritz with the crowd *at all*. If the jokes about sex weren't working, he couldn't switch to a new topic. If he was heckled, he'd just stand there and strangle. He had almost no stage skills other than plowing through his eight-minute set.

People going out tonight, he would begin. *Some go out to dinner. Some go to the comedy club. Other people wanna FUCK!* And if that got a good laugh, as it sometimes did, it usually meant that Mike would have a good set. If they laugh hard at the first line, you don't have to convince them you're funny anymore. They know, and they'll believe it for the next hour, or in Mike's case, the next few minutes. *I was in the Eaton Centre, and I was eatin' this girl out. And they threw me out! I said, 'Hey! This is the Eatin' Centre, right?" Then I went to McDonald's. I ordered a McChicken sandwich and I was McJerkin' off and they McThrew me out! I like Italian girls. I think they give the best blowjobs, because the hair on their upper lip gives it more friction.* The most innovative bit he had was a discussion of Disco. It's hard to tell the young punks today, with their rap and their hip-hop, that we, their parents, lived through a very similar period of all beat, no lyrics crapola music called disco. *I was on the Merv Griffin Show and Merv said, 'Macho Man, what do you think of disco?' And I said, 'Merv......fuck you!' Then I was on the Tonight show and Johnny Carson said to me, 'Macho Man, what do you think of disco?' And I said, 'Johnny......fuck Merv!'* Although the bit absolutely cries out for a third one, the topper, I don't think Mike had one. Either that or I can't remember what it was.

When Mike finished his set, he wouldn't say goodnight. He'd just walk off. I don't think he ever had much of an idea how he did up there, either. The rest of us were obsessed with our shows.

"How'd you do, man?"

"How'd I do? You didn't see it?"

"No man, I just got here."

"You didn't see it? Oh, I *killed.* I murdered. They screamed. You didn't see any of it?"

"No."

"Well, I destroyed. God help the poor bastard who had to follow me."

Mike didn't give a rat's ass how he did. He came down, did his set, got his $25 or whatever and went home. He never joined in any of our reindeer games. He didn't play softball or road hockey or poker, he didn't watch wrestling or go to strip clubs. At least not with us. He never went on the road, either, for obvious reasons. He only performed at Yuks and only on weekends. Mark always had a sadistic streak in him, especially when it came to the audience, and I'm fairly sure he saw Mike as a sort of living theatre piece. Mike was around probably at least five or six years. I'd come off the road time after time and see him in his '50s finery, ready to go on and give another well dressed crowd their electro-shock therapy.

Then one night I went down to the club and I saw Mike with a girl. He was dressed like a regular person as well. Plaid shirt and jeans and shoes. The only time I ever saw him in shoes. The girl was dressed like she was going to a hop, but she was cute enough. A bit of conversation showed that Mike hadn't hooked up with anyone smarter than he was, but they both had rings on, and were both beaming in their newfound happiness and love. And of course, she was pregnant. Mike introduced her around, so proud he almost busticated.

I never saw Mike again after that night. But we did hear that a baby had been born. A girl. Then a few months after that we heard that Mike and his wife had been arrested. They had abused the child, burning her with cigarettes and beating her. I think the little girl survived and Mike went to jail, which would not have been like the '50s at all.

I was depressed because I had no shoes. Then I saw a man who had no feet. And I said to him, "Hey, you must have a pair of shoes that you're not using."

MOVING OUT & UP: 1985/86

AFTER LIVING with Tony Molesworth for two years, he moved out. Soon after that, the owners of the building decided to convert all the big apartments into two smaller ones, so I moved out as well. I took a walk around the neighbourhood one day and found a place for rent on Jarvis street, a block south of Wellesely. It was a basement one bedroom with a fairly large kitchen and living room. The best thing about it was that it had a back door which led to a small stairway to the side of the building to the street. In the morning, I could get up and get the paper from the Toronto Star box on the street. Eight steps up and eight back. There were several really good food and convenience stores a block away, and I even found an underground parking garage for my car that cost, wait for it, $40 a month. At night hookers roamed my block, negotiating their assignations through car windows right in front of the building. It was decadent and cool and I loved living there.

I think I made somewhere between $20,000 and $25,000 that year. I had begun to work Michigan and the midwest states a great deal, through John Yoder, a comedy booker based in Grand Rapids. John's weeks consisted of one-nighters Tuesday, Wednesday, and Thursday, then a club in one of the larger towns on Friday and Saturday, and sometimes a Sunday one-nighter. The larger towns were Toledo,

Grand Rapids, Kalamazoo, Lansing, Jackson, Madison, and South Bend. The smaller towns were everything else. Owosso, Big Rapids, Spring Lake, Benton Harbor, Flint, Mount Pleasant, Grand Haven, Traverse City, Ann Arbor, Saginaw, Holly, Muskegon, Ludington, Green Bay, Appleton, Beloit, Steven's Point, Rockford, West Lafayette, Mishiwaka, and that's as far as my memory goes today. Amazingly, none of them were really that bad. Most were college towns, and in those days college students still had something resembling an attention span.

I worked with a lot of great American acts in those days. John Connell became a trusted friend. A former pool hustler, who went by the moniker, 'Corn' for his sandy hair, John was a fine comedian and an extraordinary storyteller. He would have been a great confidence man. He could talk his way into an operating theatre without scrubs or a mask. He once phoned the most exclusive golf club in Kalamazoo, The Moors, and, identifying himself as 'Doctor Connell, he told the pro he had a friend in from Los Angeles (me), and he wanted to show him the best golf course in the midwest. If it wasn't too busy today could we come and play? It being a Tuesday, the pro invited me and the Doctor to come down. On the way there, John instructed me not to blanch at any price we might be charged, and to act as though I was a guy from L.A. with dough to spend.

"And for God's sake don't say 'ooot' the way you Canadians do or he'll know you're not from L.A. Look, just try and keep your mouth shut as much as possible until we get to the first green."

John's advice was always excellent. He was a hell of a golfer as well. From his hustler days, he retained an amazing ability to produce his best shots when the money was on the line. We didn't play big money, a dollar a hole, with carryovers. He'd shoot 81, I'd shoot 82, and I'd lose $18. It was unbelievable. I once beat him by three shots and lost $16. But I didn't care — much. He made me laugh. We were playing a par-five hole once and I was on in two, putting for eagle. John had a 120-yard uphill, partially blind shot for his third, and he knew he had to get it close to keep the pressure on me. He hit it up there and I saw it land on the green and called back to him, "You're dancing." meaning he was on the dance floor, the green. When we got closer, it was apparent that he was within three feet of the hole.

"Dancing?" he cried. "*Dancing?* I'm sucking the bandleader's *dick!* He's tapping me on the head with his stick!"

John was a dedicated pot smoker. So much so that he had a technique that enabled him to smoke pot in a crowded bar and never get caught. You had to have a cigarette going and the pot had to be in a little pipe. He would put the cigarette in the ashtray, surreptitiously light the pipe and take a deep draw of the marijuana. When he was finished, he immediately covered the bowl of the pipe with a matchbook, so no smoke could escape. Then, with the pot smoke still in his lungs, he'd take a drag on the cigarette and blow everything out, the two vapours mixing to cover up the smell. I told him about my way of saving a joint. I would take a drag on the joint, then hold it at the bottom of an upside down glass perched on the edge of a table. The smoke that was released while I was holding my first drag would go up into the glass. Then I would turn it over and suck up that smoke as well. Efficient. It's lovely to remember how egregiously stupid you were when you set your inquiring mind to the task of finding better ways to fuck yourself up.

Steve Iott was another comic I saw a lot of in those years. A Michigan boy, married and divorced young, he drifted into comedy and was very good at it. A somewhat bitter man, like me, his jokes had a really sharp edge.

My buddy Ernie keeps bugging me to let him drive my car, but I'm not gonna. I can't let him drive because he's a midget. Not that I have anything against midgets. My best friend Ernie happens to be a midget. But I can't let him drive my car. He's so short that the only way he can drive is by watching the expression on the passenger's face.

I met Carla Filisha on a Yoder tour. She was from Chicago, all of four feet ten inches tall, looked like she was a cute eleven year old, but underneath she could swear like a sailor and was tougher than anyone I'd met. Funny as hell, too. I started staying at her place in Chicago on my off days between Yoder runs. She took me to see the Biograph Theatre, which was a couple of blocks from her apartment. John Dillinger had been gunned down there in 1933 after watching Clark Gable go to the electric chair in *Manhattan Melodrama*. Always better to die coming out of a good movie, feeling good, as opposed to being riddled with bullets while standing in line to buy a ticket. I took a photo of the theatre. I took a lot of photos then. Mostly in graveyards.

I had picked up the habit of visiting graveyards from driving a lot of back roads to get to Yoder gigs. I began to scour the Baseball Encyclopedia for information on dead ballplayers, and started making little side trips to get certain graves. We always did radio promotions in the larger towns, which meant hauling your ass out of bed between six and seven a.m. and being 'funny' for a morning show.

I began to ask listeners to call in if they knew where anyone interesting was buried. If that didn't work, I'd phone the local boneyards and ask the caretaker about residents. I supplemented the information by personally checking any small graveyards I saw by the road, provided I wasn't in a hurry to get to a job. My original goal was to photograph the graves of the eight Black Sox, the ballplayers who were tossed out of baseball for throwing the 1919 World Series. I ended up getting only four, although I know where three others are. I just haven't been booked in or near those towns. It was a great hobby. I did it seriously for about ten years. I have a photo album with over 300 photos that range from Bonnie and Clyde to Laurel and Hardy. I loved the history of it, the calm, leafy atmosphere of most cemeteries, and the fact that doing it added to my reputation as an odd, intense sort of guy.

The summer of 1985 brought me my first Montreal Comedy Festival. One of the women booking comedians that year was Kandi Abelson, who I knew from her time in Toronto. She knew all of us and tried to book all of us that year. It was the second year of the English festival. Mike MacDonald, Ron Vaudry, me, and Larry Horowitz were the comics from Toronto. Among the American acts were Dom Irrera, Joe Bolster, Pete Barbutti, Jerry Seinfeld, and some guy named Jay Leno. It was also the year that Quebec native Andre-Phillippe Gagnon made his debut, wowing the crowd with his rendition of 'We Are The World', doing all the voices. It was a heady week, full of marijuana and cocaine and parties and comedians talking to each other. I had never been so happy.

My gala show at Theatre St. Denis went very well. I did 'Comedy's Better' and my Neil Young song. You can still see it once in a while on the Comedy Network. I look really young (I was not quite 26) and I'm wearing my standard stage outfit of the period. Black dress pants, black shoes, a dress shirt and tie, and a wine-coloured, sleeveless golf vest that my mother bought me when I was seventeen. At rehearsal, I was intimidated by the enormous proscenium of the St. Denis, and I wondered how the hell I would fill that space up. But I did a great show. Lucky, because it was the first thing I ever did that was taped for television. It had been five years and two weeks since my Amateur Night debut. I met Jay Leno that night. He came backstage and said hello to everyone. When he saw Jerry Seinfeld's name on the show list, done in big red marker, Jay borrowed a marker from a stagehand and wrote *who?* next to Jerry's name.

I was so nervous backstage that I was completely paranoid. Larry Horowitz came over to me a few minutes before I went on and offered me a glass of water. I took one sip and suddenly realized that I couldn't trust Larry. Who knew what that bastard might have put in the drink? I put it down and didn't take anymore. A huge mistake. First of all, Larry was the *one* guy you could trust in any random group of comics, and secondly, two jokes into the set I got the worst case of dry mouth I'd ever had. When I showed my teeth, I could feel my top lip sticking to my gums, making me leer like a rabbit. But I managed to get through the set and do well. Afterward, someone gave me a Lifesaver, which I sucked on for about 15 minutes. When I took it out of my mouth, you could still read the word, 'Lifesaver' on it. (That's a joke). I followed Ron Vaudry, who did a lousy set. He was in front of his hometown crowd but he tried to do a 'cool' set, and they weren't buying. That night, at a party at the Hotel Du Parc – the best hotel I had stayed in up to that time – Ron and I were talking to Mike MacDonald, whose gala was the next night. Mike asked us how it had gone.

"The theatre's so big," said Ron, "It's hard to hear the laughs." It didn't seem to bother Mike, but it bothered me. If you go up on any show thinking it's going to suck, baby, *it's going to suck*. No question. I took Mike aside a bit later and gave him my opinion.

"Listen, you'll be able to hear the laughs. Ron didn't hear any because he wasn't getting any." Mike nodded. I think he knew anyway. Ron looked up to Mike something fierce in those days. One night, Mike had just come back from a trip to the States and he'd brought a video of himself performing in Florida for us to watch. He got everybody stoned and insisted we watch the tape. About 40 minutes into his hour and twenty minute show, Mike started doing Ron's act! And he wasn't stupid. He would have known it was on there and Ron was going to watch it. Ron didn't like it, but he was subdued about it. Normally, he was Mr. Let's-fight, Mr. Don't-fuck-with-me, but he never said boo to Mike. Later, someone who was there said, "I never knew Ron's act was funny until I saw Mike do it."

I did my last show at that festival at Le Spectrum, on the bill with Jay Leno. My sister took a picture of me that afternoon, standing outside the place. I was pointing up to my name on the marquee, and a guy on a ladder was finishing up the names. He was putting the 'n' in Leno. Jay watched my set that night and complimented me on my Madonna bit. I would sing the first couple of lines to 'Like A Virgin', and then stop and say, *"Come on, don't you believe it more when I do it?"* It was the culmination of five years of hard work, and I truly felt that I'd arrived.

It wasn't until months later that I heard through back channels that most of the American acts had thought I was an asshole. A punk kid hanging onto their coattails. It still stings to think of it. I eventually became friends with Dom Irrera, got to know Jay Leno a little bit, and even auditioned for the part of George Costanza on 'Seinfeld'. Didn't get it though. I may have been an asshole, but I wasn't *that* big an asshole.

I STARTED DATING an actress in the fall of 1985. Her name was Kate, and I put a lot of effort into courting her. She was at first reluctant to go out with the likes of me, an instinct she probably should have paid more attention to. I had dated a few women after Judy and I split up. I thought it ended for religious reasons – she being Jewish and I not-Jewish – but as the years passed, I suspected it had more to do with my astounding immaturity and deep-rooted self-absorption, both much-needed qualities for the successful comedian, but perilous in other aspects of life. I generally got bored very quickly with the women I dated. Once I bedded them, their days were usually numbered. Kate was different. She refused to be drawn into my little web for the longest time, which gave our relationship a chance, I suppose. Finally I prevailed, and in December of 1985, we decided to move in together. We had found an apartment in the St. Clair-Avenue Road area of Toronto. A nice little place with a loft bedroom. I'd given the landlord a cheque for first and last month's rent. I was due to go on tour in New York and Massachusetts for a week, and was on my way to do my banking the next morning, twenty-four hours before Lawrence Morgenstern and I would be heading out. I stopped at the Yuk Yuks office to check on my January and February bookings. Connie Winkleman had bollixed them up, which was normal, I suppose, but for some reason, this screw-up enraged me. By then I was very meticulous about bookings. Maybe the office staff didn't know that. When my tirade was over, they knew it much better. After swearing at the very top of my lungs a couple of times, I headed for the glass door and slapped it open. It shattered and I went through it rather than around it. I kept walking. A few steps to the stairs going down to Bay Street and I noticed the blood. All over my pants. I had gouged a deep chunk out of the heel of my right hand. I went to my car and drove immediately to Wellesely Hospital. At the emergency desk, I only had to show them my hand to get immediate service. It took 17 stitches to fix it, but I was lucky. No major tendons or nerves had been hit. I was lucky I hadn't slashed my wrist and bled to death on the way to the car. I returned to Yuks after the stitching, still somewhat in shock, and apologized for exploding like that. The door was already boarded and the booking snafu magically fixed. And, on the good side, they never screwed up another booking of mine again. On the bad side, I never did get to the bank, so as a result, the cheque for the apartment bounced. But that was a few days later, and by then I was in my car somewhere. In New England.

Lawrence and I drove to Binghampton, New York, the next day, and he headlined because I couldn't play the guitar. My hand was quite intricately bandaged, and I enjoyed changing the bandage every few hours. The stitches were in place, but the cut was so deep that it bled continually for several days. The second night we were in Oneonta, NY. It was only five miles or so from Cooperstown, so I spent the afternoon at the Baseball Hall of Fame, buying remaindered 1984 Detroit Tiger merchandise. It was the only touristy thing I did that trip.

Thursday we were in Falmouth, and I decided to play the guitar, or at least attempt it. I managed to get through the show, but my bandage was blood-soaked when it was over. After I changed it, I called home, and got the news that we'd lost the apartment the day before. Kate hadn't been able to get me on the phone, and had phoned a number of people in a panic. I got some amazing tales of her hysterical reaction over the next few weeks. "Man your girlfriend called me one night....hooo eee!" It didn't bother me that we'd lost the place. There were hundreds of places to live in Toronto.

Friday Lawrence and I hit old Boston, where we played Nick's Comedy Stop. Lawrence spent the afternoon in the 'Combat Zone' the drugs-and-hookers area of town. It was the only touristy thing he did that trip. The next night, Saturday, we were in Waterville, Maine. However, in trying to extricate ourselves from Boston, we got in the wrong lane and I had a stupidity-while-driving episode that resulted in a fender bender that ruined my driver's side headlight. It cost us an extra hour listening to the guy we ran into, whose vehicle had not one scratch, tell us what complete dinks we were. Or maybe what a complete dink I was. Sunday we were back in Lowell, Mass. for a bar gig.

I was so tired of the job, and also weary of hanging with Lawrence, so I suggested we hump it back to Toronto in one haul after the show in Lowell. It was the first time I'd ever done that, and I liked it so much it became my habit.

Kate and I found another apartment in Parkdale, on Wilson Park Road. It was the bottom floor of a house, and we ended up living there for eight months.

My car eventually got a new headlight, but the frame was bent from the Boston accident and the headlight shone downward so it wasn't any damn good, really. It's amazing that I wasn't in more accidents then, because I was a truly horrible driver. I had trouble staying in my lane, I was always nervous, I panicked a lot, and I drove stoned a good deal of the time. Someone was watching over me, I suppose. I had to use my high-beams all the time at night or I could barely see anything, so the other drivers didn't like me much. They honked and flashed their high-beams at me all the time. But I kept driving. Working for John Yoder was a driving occupation. I liked John, mostly because of one episode in our relationship. John was booking the Toledo Comedy Club for most of 1985, until he had a falling out with the owner, one Alan Sedar. Alan called me after he and John had parted, and offered me the gig at better money than John used to pay. I took it. A few days later I got a call from John.

"Did you book a week at the Toledo Comedy Club?" he asked. I allowed that I had done so.

"You know that guy's an asshole, right? He screwed me. He screwed me out of $3,000. I wish you wouldn't work for a scumbag like that."

"I'm sorry, John." What the hell else could I say? There was a long pause over the line, and then finally I heard John again.

"So, you wanna book some dates?"

"Absolutely." How could you not like a guy like that? Mark Breslin would have said cancel the Toledo date or you'll never work for me again. And I would have canceled it. In a heartbeat. But John understood that business is business (and Christmas is bullshit) . This was my living. I'd book the club he was no longer affiliated with, and I'd do his shit-money little Michigan/Ohio tours. I was starting to get a great return on American money at home, so I didn't care what they paid me. Remember, I was a professional fool.

The best John Yoder story happened with Steve Iott. Steve called John for some dates and was having trouble hearing him because there was a lot of noise in the background.

"The job is five nights in a row and pays $550, total," said John. "That's summer money, of course. I sorry, but I can't do any better." *Summer money* was one of John's great whines. The crowds were smaller in summer because the college towns always lay dormant until September. People liked to be outdoors when the weather was nice, too, rather than being stuck in a black-on-black basement comedy room. So John made the same money but the comics got less. Steve thought he might be able to squeeze some blood out of the turnip.

"Could I get an extra hundred, John? For gas money? It's four days of driving."

"I'm sorry, man," said John, "It's summer, man. I just can't do it."

How about an extra fifty then? Just for gas."

"I'm really sorry Stevie. It's summer, man. I just can't do it."

"An extra twenty-five then. It's *four* days driving, John."

"I can't do it, man. It's summer. It's summer money. I can't do it."

"John, what the hell is that awful noise?

"Oh. That's a backhoe. They're building my pool."

Two guys sitting on a park bench, middle of the day. Dog walks by, lies down in front of the bench. Dog reaches down, takes both of his testicles into his mouth, gives 'em a good lick. One guy turns to the other and says, "Sure wish I could do that." The other guy says, "He'd bite you."

YEAR OF THE DOG: 1986

It TAKES FIVE years to become a real comedian. You have to do between three and five hundred shows before you have any sense of what it's about, and you have to write enough material to fill a novel. I actually thought of my act as a living novel that I carried around with me like a salesman. Once or twice a day I'd open my sample case and read my novel aloud. Another great thing was that after five years, you didn't stop learning. Your act grew with you, assuming you were capable of growth. Your knowledge grew. You weren't merely a performer of comedy anymore; you began to be someone who understood it. My lines started getting shorter. I could find the swiftest path to the jokes now. My persona became more natural. I could walk on *knowing* how it was going to go. That takes a lot of shows. In 1986, I did 282 shows, at an average stipend of $113. I had gone, in four years, from making next to nothing to making $30,000.

One of the things I loved was the timing. I had never worn a watch, but I learned how to time my show. In Rochester, there was a clock visible where I stood before I was introduced. Just before my name was called, I would note the time, and nothing gave me more pleasure than finishing the show, walking off an noting that I'd been up there 45 minutes, within a minute or so. One night I checked the minute hand of the clock, and when I finished, I calculated that I'd done a show of forty-five minutes and three seconds. You need an hour? I can do an hour. You need 52 minutes? No problem. Just give me a light at forty-nine and a half.

I had full command of the microphone by then as well, which sounds easy, but it isn't. It took many years of experimenting with styles to get the way I was most comfortable, which was the mike in my left hand, elbow bent and locked to the side of my body. Shoulder and arm and mike all moving as one so the mike is always in the same place, just under my chin. I always knew where it was, and could subtly move my head forward or back to modulate the sound. I know it sounds trivial, but watch a comedian with no mike technique and you'll understand the importance.

I had all my hosting tricks to use. I could fool around with the audience if I had to and handle virtually all heckles. In fact, and please don't spread this around, I *liked* a crowd that was a bit raucous. An energetic group with a couple of mouthy but good-natured women near the front was my favourite. Naturally, saying such things can get you in trouble. I worked in Halifax for the first time in 1985, a two-week stint at the Privateer's Warehouse. The act before me was a folksinger named John Gracie, and it was such a pleasure to go to work and hear John play and sing. I stayed in a band house with the group working the room upstairs. The Micah Barnes Band, as I recall. The day we left for home there was a new band moving in. K.D. Lang and the ReClines. But I digress. One night late in the second week, a reporter from Canadian Press came to see the show and interview me. It happened to be a really rowdy group that evening and I had my hands full keeping the show on track. The reporter brought that up immediately, but I shrugged it off, saying it wasn't a bother at all. Sometimes it even helped the energy of a show. Well, stupid me. (*Stupid Me* was originally going to be the title of this book) The article came out all across the damn country with the headline: *HECKLERS ESSENTIAL TO COMIC*. Sheeee-it! In the local paper, the last line of the piece said, *"So come on down to the Warehouse this weekend and give comedian John Wing a piece of your mind."* Or words to that effect.

But as long as I wasn't being interviewed, I could handle most things. I had a shocking realization near the beginning of the year. Briane Nasimok had said I would bomb some night and realize they were wrong, and then I'd be a comedian. But one night in 1986 I killed and realized the audience was wrong. I wasn't on the stick that night for whatever reason, but *they hadn't noticed.* I could do a show that seemed great but I knew was substandard. I started kicking ass on my off nights as well as the nights where I was hot. The reason had a lot to do with a couple of little jokes someone told me in the latter part of 1985.

I don't recall where or who it was who told me. It could have been a cab driver. They were always telling me jokes. But I came into possession of two dumb little jokes. *Where do you find a dog with no legs? Right where you left him.* And *What do you call a dog with no legs. No use callin' him.* They weren't unknown to other comics. I just found a use for them. The last part of my act, the musical part, was the weakest then. I had eight or ten musical pieces, mostly short parodies, closing with The Breakup Song, bu there was no structure to them. No thread. One night I remembered the two dog jokes as I was going into the musical portion of the set, so I tossed one in there. It killed. So I did the other one. It killed, too. So I did them the next show. And the next. The musical act was still adding and shedding pieces, but I had started to open it with a Bryan Adams song called 'Heaven'.

Baby you're all that I want,
When you're lying here in my arms,
I'm finding it hard to believe,
You're eleven......(spoken) Don't you hate that? You know, they say they're
twelve. They look twelve, lying like that? The kids today. No moral code.

Then I had a Bruce Springsteen parody I'd written with Steve Iott on a Yoder run in Wisconsin. The song was called 'Fire'.

I'm riding in your car, you turn on the radio.
You're pulling me close, I just say no.
You say 'Why don't you like it?'
And I say, 'Cause, you're a guy.'
But when we kiss...oooh, oooh, ewwww, yecchh (Hawk, spit) What is that,
Skoal? Jesus! (Spit and spit again) Take me home Walt. Prom night's over.

Then another Bryan Adams parody which embarrassment forces me to omit from this text, and so on, and so on. One of the great things about musical bits is that they all need intros, and those intros should always be funny. There should be extros as well, easing out of the bit and into the next one. Always in keeping with the logic of the parody.

So I was trying to write funny intros and extros, although many of them happened spontaneously when I was up onstage. Spontaneity is wonderful, but you can never count on it. (Unless, like Robin Williams, you have fooled your ignorant audience into thinking that the lowest-common-denominator crap you have stolen comes off the top of your head.) I would put the songs in one order one night, and then another the next night, getting a feel for the pairings that worked best. Then, one night on a western tour in early 1986, I sat down at the desk in my hotel room and started to write dog-with-no-legs jokes.

What do you call a dog with no legs in heat? Shit out of luck.

Where do you take a dog with no legs? The dragstrip. This was a variation on the joke, "I have a dog with no legs. Every night I take him out for a drag." Variations became very important to the bit because I never wanted audience members to be able to yell out answers to the wholly rhetorical setup questions.

What do you feed a dog with no legs? Meals on Wheels. Okay. That's not bad. Now what? So I'd sit there, thinking of any dog variations, or dog traits, or words that go with dog until I came to one I could phrase into a question.

What do you call a dog with no legs on a barbecue? Frank.

How does a dog with no legs do a bellyflop? Perfectly.

What kind of job can a dog with no legs get in a bar? Bouncer. Imagining it visually gave me the bellyflop joke, so I went back to the water.

What do you get when you throw a dog with no legs in the water? Four or five skips, but you've gotta know exactly how to do it. Another variation, the original being "What do call a dog with no legs in the water? Bob." A lot of audience members knew that one, so I needed a good twist on it. Now back to the idea. What do I know about dogs? What do dog trainers always say......?

How do you make a dog with no legs cry? Tell him, "Stay." I like that. That'll work well. Now back to the drag joke. There's something else there. Come on. You're walking the dog, you're walking the....

How do you walk a dog with no legs? Hit him with the first pitch. Oh, that's good. I like that one a lot. What else have we got? A dog with no legs is what? An ugly woman, right? Hey.....

What do you call a dog with no legs in Russia? Mrs. Gorbachev. Later it was Mrs. Yeltsin, and then I moved it to Washington and it became 'Hillary', and now it's in Ottawa and the answer is, 'Mrs. Chretien.' Time flies. Let's get one more. Come on, just one, right? Now what can you do to a dog? What can you....

How do you fuck a dog with no legs? I was drunk.

There were a few others. I think I wrote 10 or 12 that day. Not all of them were right for the show, but I started throwing them in. The first two, the ones I'd heard from someone, had started killing, so I wasn't scared to do more of them. And the piece evolved, almost imperceptibly.

I would start with *Where do you find a dog with no legs? Right where you left him. He hasn't moved. Trust me.* Very slight pauses between the lines. Then Bryan Adams number one. I would ask the crowd, *Any Bryan Adams fans?* (applause) *Good, I'm into acne-rock.* That just came swimming out of my head one night and never left. Do the song about the 11-year-old whore, and then the next dog joke. *What do you call a dog with no legs? No use callin' him. He hasn't moved, he's not coming.* Then the Springsteen parody, then the shit-out-of-luck joke, which seguéed nicely in Bryan Adams number two, which was a parody of the song 'Run To You', which dealt with diarrhea. I added some tags to the shit joke. *What do you call a dog with no legs in heat? Shit out of luck. Come on, he's half-cocked. He's a teeter-totter. Who the hell's going to sleep with him?* Performed at full speed. No pauses. In the beginning weeks of the piece, I was adding little things almost every night. Okay, so after 'Run To You', then *Where do you take a dog with no legs? The dragstrip.* And the possibilities there intrigued me as well. Taking a dog to a dragstrip, eh? What else might happen? The extro became, *Hey, my dog loves it. He goes whipping down that track — big parachute comes out of his ass at the end. Whoooeeee! It's a good time, for everybody except the guy who has to pack it. "What? And leave show business?"* And it's just logic. Dragsters have parachutes that deploy after the race, and parachutes have to be packed, albeit not up a dog's ass, but you get the idea. That tag was the most important, because it added the first new layer to the bit.

Each dog line thereafter would be more than a joke. It would be an adventure.

I wrote a parody of the Kinks' song, 'Lola', which went next. It was pretty much the same as their song, except when Lola said her name, I did it in my deepest, growliest voice, and then, for once breaking the parody rule that once you get to the joke, STOP!, I went on to add,

Well, I'm not the world's most passionate guy
But when she showed me her dick, well, I kinda went wild for Lola...

Also, I'd added a line after 'Run To You' which was *Hey, if I'd known you liked diarrhea jokes, I would have put em in earlier in the show! You should have said something.* So after 'Lola', I started saying *Hey, if I'd known you liked transvestism jokes, I would have dressed differently for the show.* Layers. The first just mentions that we did a diarrhea joke. The second, a callback, cuts it deeper, going into the cross-dressing topic in a little more detail. This was the second running gag in the piece. One night I went into 'Lola' and asked first if there were any Kinks' fans? The response was mediocre, only a few people. *Okay, cool. Now, how about the band The Kinks'?* Another permanent resident found. The intro for 'Lola' was the last part written for the bit. Each bit had its text, then its intro, extro, etc. Other than writing the actual parody first, you never knew when the dressing jokes would appear. But they would.

After the Kinks bit came the joke *What do you feed a dog with no legs?* By now the crowd is getting used to the rhythm of it. Musical bit –

dog joke – musical bit – dog joke, so they're getting a little lethargic. Time to wake them up. *Meals On Wheels! Or ground beef. Whatever you decide. I like to give you a choice, knowing you're going to be telling these at home all next week.*

One night in Victoria, B.C. I must have had the entire ASPCA in the audience because they were seriously offended by my dog jokes and I was getting a bit nervous. Lucky for me, though. Encountering this crowd provided one of the keys to the whole bit. I backtracked at a couple of points that show, saying things like, *Gee, I sure hope I'm not offending you guys with these dog jokes...*which got a couple of okay laughs. Nothing special, and I wasn't thinking too much about it when, after the show, one of the other comics suggested that apologizing for offending them was really funny. So the third layer was born. The apologies. I started to apologize after Meals on Wheels, acting as though it had just occurred to me that some might be offended by such humour. *Gosh, I sure hope I'm not offending anybody with this dog material. If we have dog owners, or animals lover, or Martha Stewart fans, I sure don't want to offend. So let's get off this dog thing. I think it's time. Let's get into something a little more...sophisticated...intellectual . Neil Young? Any Neil Young fans? Who cares? I'm gonna do him anyway.*

The original TV personality was not Martha Stewart, but I can't remember who I used. A well-known animal lover. Bridget Bardot, maybe. It was a nice one-two-three joke. Where I came up with sophisticated and intellectual I don't know, but they both stuck. Then I would do Neil Young, with my ridiculous smoke-damaged-furniture falsetto, which made for the inevitable, *Hey, if I'd known you liked castration jokes, I would have cut 'em in earlier. Hey, come on now. I could have said 'sliced'.* Then short pause, perhaps a sip of my drink, and we're back. *What do you call a dog with no legs on a barbecue? Frank. Or Patty, if it's a bitch.* Then, adding another tiny layer, I would laugh at my dog joke. This is generally not done, it being the mark of a bad comedian, but it can be done for effect. Garry Shandling always did it better than anyone I saw. But, as my laugh trailed off, I would realize something. *Oh gosh, I sure hope I didn't offend anybody with that barbecue joke. If we have barbecue enthusiasts here, I wouldn't want to offend the briquet crowd, or the mesquite crowd. I understand they've split into two crowds. If there are any bitches named Patty in the audience, I am sorry. Let's get off this dog thing. I think it's time. Let's get into something a little more...sophisticated...intellectual. Any Gordon Lightfoot fans? Really?? No kidding, you really are? Okay, for the fan.*

I can see her lying back in her satin dress,
But she's dead and I killed her and I'm in a mess.
Somehow I'll make the cops understand,
I was shaving with my switchblade and she fell on my hand.

Years later, I was able to sneak an O.J. joke into the tag for this song. *If I'd known you liked O.J. jokes....etc.*

So, we're seven or eight bits into the musical set and we've got three gags running. The dog jokes, the if-I'd-known-you-liked jokes, and the apology. And we're not even close to being done. *What do you get when you kick a dog with no legs? Three points.* (laughing, hard) *Three points! Three po...*(trailing off) *three of them. Gosh I sure hope I didn't offend anybody with that field goal joke. If we have* (insert name of local football team here) *fans, I wouldn't want to offend you...any MORE. Let's get off this dog thing. I think it's time. Let's get into something a little more sophisticated... intellectual. How about a little Oak Ridge Boys?*

My baby is American made,
Nylon hair and a lifelike face
And she doesn't talk much but she sure can inflate.
My baby is American made........Yeah, I dated an inflatable woman once. On the box it said, 'Totally Lifelike'. Was, too. Blew her up. She left me.

Chris Finn, a Toronto comic who later wrote for MadTV and This Hour Has 22 Minutes, gave me that joke. It never worked for him. He looked like a guy who got laid now and then. I didn't. The same thing as that Bible joke and Geechy Guy. It worked for Geech because he played a dumbo onstage. I couldn't make an audience believe I wouldn't know the commandments. But I could always make 'em believe I was sexually inadequate. That was a cinch.

So, back to the dogs. The bellyflop joke would go next, and I would laugh even harder, allowing the laugh to taper off until I realized that I had again offended them. *Gosh I sure hope I didn't offend anybody with that bellyflop joke. If we have Greg Louganis fans, I sure wouldn't want to offend. Let's get off this dog thing. I think it's time.* (Now they are beginning to anticipate the next few lines. There is a comfort in these lines in that I always say them the same way. It lulls the crowd into thinking they know what I'm doing) *Let's get into something a little more...sophisticated...intellectual. Something we can all relate to on a culturally literate level.*

Just sit right back and you'll hear a tale, a tale of a fateful trip
That started from this tropic port, aboard this tiny ship.
The mate was a homosexual, the skipper a big fat slob,
And that's why they got shipwrecked,
Cause nobody could do their fucking job.

I was too embarrassed to write out the second Bryan Adams song, but I have to give you this real piece of crap comedy, although it still embarrasses me. Its only two laughs come from a stupid, gratuitous gay joke, and the judicious insertion of the word 'fucking'. But, it always got a huge response. So fuck you. And I would say, *Ahhh, a Gilligan-conscious crowd. If I'd known you liked bad parodies of bad TV shows....how about a singalong? You guys up for a singalong?*

Now for the first time in the set, two musical bits are going to go back to back. This is significant. It's the first major rhythm change. The reason is I want to put a little distance between me and the last dog joke. Just a little... *it's a pretty easy singalong. I'll be singing. And at certain points in the song, I'll step away from the mike, like this. That's your cue to come whippin' in with your part of the song. Think you can handle that? Good. 'Cause I'm not even telling you what song we're doing. But when I do this* (Step away from mike, in Elvis-lean-style pose) *That's your cue. Here we go.* And I would play the theme song of the cartoon, 'Underdog', the only super hero whose name meant, 'favoured to lose'.

When in this world the headlines read
Of those whose hearts are filled with greed
And rob and steal from those who need

To right this wrong with blinding speed goes UNDERDOG (Underdog)
UNDERDOG (Underdog)
Speed of lightning, power of thunder
Fighting those who rob or plunder
(Underdog), oh,oh,oh,oh,oh, (Underdog),
UN–DER–DOG!!

The audience had only to sing the three syllable, 'Underdog', and they usually did it very well. If they didn't get into it, I would end it a little early and say, *"That sucked."* Always have a contingency plan. But normally it was a truly exhilarating number. I would take a moment afterward, and then... *Speaking of dogs, as we were only a moment ago.* It would get a big laugh simply because of the distance. The surprise. *What do you get when you throw a dog with no legs in the water? Four or five skips, but you gotta know exactly how to do it. You gotta get down low there, and really SNAP that wrist, really snap it. Oh gosh,* (And by now, merely saying 'Oh gosh' is getting the laugh) *I sure hope I didn't offend anyone with that rock-skipping joke. If we have rock skipping enthusiasts here....get a job. Really, it's worth the money. Hey, Let's get off this dog thing. I think it's time. Let's get into something a little more...*and like good little Pavlovians, they're yelling it out, Sophisticated! Intellectual! in a perfect, conditioned response scenario. And I would say...*Hey, whatever you guys want. I'm your whore. Plumb my depths. Little more sophisticated, you say? Neil Diamond? Any Neil Diamond fans? Yeah? I had a feeling he still sold here.*

You are the sand, I am the pail,
You are the dog, I am the tail,

Wag me. Wag me baby. Wag me harder.
A couple more wags oughtta do it.

And then another *Hey, speaking of dogs,* leading into *How do you make a dog with no legs cry? You tell him, "Stay." "Stay right there."* And then no laughing anymore, but a resigned sort of *oh shit, I hope I didn't offend anybody there, with that 'Stay' joke. If we have Barbara Woodhouse fans, I sure wouldn't want to.....ahh the hell with it.* By now, if you change the runners, it almost doesn't matter what you say. Anything different will be surprising enough to get a laugh. *How do you walk a dog with no legs? Hit him with the first pitch. Come on, he's crowding the plate. Plunk him. Shave him. A little snout music! What's he gonna do, charge the mound? I seriously doubt it. Is anyone offended by that? Okay then, what do you call a dog with no legs in Russia. Mrs. Gorbachev.* (Groans, always) *Oh gosh, I hope I didn't offend any COMMUNISTS out there!* For a while I did a really offensive joke in the next spot. *What do you say to a mongoloid dog with no legs? Down, Syndrome!* One night a woman came up after the show, smiling, which was always dangerous. I was never sure if they wanted to fuck me or berate me for my misogyny, or my anti-religious jokes, or just to introduce me to her husband. But this woman came up and said, "I just wanted to tell you how much I enjoyed the show. And I have a Down's Syndrome child. And I still loved the show." I never did the joke again.

In Las Vegas a few years later, I was doing a joke about alcoholism. *I don't like to say that alcoholism runs in my family. Because it gallops.* (Movie buffs will realize I stole that joke from Frank Capra's *Arsenic and Old Lace*) *We have so many heavy drinkers that suicide isn't considered a problem at our house. It's more of a holiday tradition. You know, you walk into the bathroom Christmas eve and...*(looking up) *Hey, Uncle Bill....* Then I would sway from side to side, indicating that Uncle Bill had hanged himself in the shower. *Uncle Bill?.....Hey, can I have your room?* After the show one night I got a letter from a woman who was in Vegas with her husband, trying to get over the hanging suicide of their son. That one really depressed me, but I kept doing the joke. I still have the letter, too.

Now, where were we? Oh, right. Then I would ask if there were any dog owners in the audience, pick one out and have a short chat about their dog, from which I could usually wring some laughter. Of course I only did it so I could naturally bring up my dog. *I have a dog, yeah. His name is 'Sled'. Yeah, he lost his legs last year. That's when I changed his name. Originally I called him 'Rosebud', but I felt 'Sled' fit better after the accident. Bizarre accident, too. He was playing Trivial Pursuit in the back of this Vietnamese restaurant one night, and I guess they asked him a couple of pretty tough questions. Cause he came home stumped.* That always got a huge response, be it laughs or groans. It was groans, I'd say, *Yeah? YOU write a better ending!* The word ending was important. Again I was trying to suggest that the dog bit was over. They could relax. *Hendrix? Any Hendrix fans? Elrod Hendricks, great catcher for the Orioles? This is Jimi Hendrix plays the Beverly Hillbillies theme.* Doing the Hendrix bit, which was more of an applause bit than anything else, got me a perfect segué into drugs. I brought back the killing of my cat while on acid, renaming the cat 'Fluffy'. *Which led to the tag line, Yeah, Sled bounced over and tried to help...but...*

I would close with the Breakup Song, asking afterward, *How do you fuck a dog with no legs? I was drunk. What does a dog with no legs say after sex? Comedy's Better.* That brought the act to a perfect circle, the last joke calling back the very first bit.

It took the better part of a year to get all those ducks in line. In the autumn of 1986, I was working in Ottawa with Juri Strenge (pronounced Yuri Strange, the best goddamn natural name I ever heard for a comic), and he'd become a friend. We both loved doing comedy and smoking dope, which seemed like a hell of a basis for a friendship in those days. Juri came up to me after a show one night and sang me a version of America's *Horse With No Name.* "You see, I've been through the desert on a dog with no legs...." It went into the act the very next night, following the Breakup Song, and never left.

By the end of 1986, I could do the last 25 to 28 minutes of my act in my sleep, it was so ingrained. I had achieved a consistency of performance that was pretty good considering all the dope and cigarettes I consumed, and the hours I kept. Someone was always watching over me. It was too bad they couldn't have watched over Juri as well. A couple of years after I left for Los Angeles, he was on his way to a gig in Kingston and a motorcyclist crossed the line. Juri killed the guy. An accident, for sure, and the other guy's fault, too. But there was some controversy over whether Juri was sober. They charged him with some form of vehicular homicide. I still feel horrible that I never called or visited him. It was like that in the job. When somebody left, you never went looking for him. Juri did his time, (eight months) and got out, but he never went back to stand-up, which I feel worse about because he could have been great. I still owe him for the joke he gave me, and I still know without a doubt that it could have been me driving the car that night. It's like that old joke Johnny Carson loved, the newspaper ad for the lost dog. *Speaking of dogs, as we were only a moment ago...*

LOST DOG
Terrier, black,
One eye, no tail.
Three legs.
Answers to Lucky.

Jeremy Hotz and I actually liked each other, I think. But he gave me a nickname which reflected how I was seen. He called me 'Bastard'. Not 'The Bastard', just 'Bastard'. Although the name never really caught on with everyone, he has never stopped using it as his greeting for me. I loved it then and still do. I even sewed the word onto the back of my Yuk Yuks sweatshirt. I suppose I liked it because I believed you had to be a bastard just to get by. You were going to be rejected and you couldn't take it personally, you just had to assume that the rejector was a stupid ass, and the next time he saw you he'd realize his mistake. It crept into all parts of my life, however, and made it difficult to maintain certain relationships. My nickname never really caught on with my colleagues, but virtually all my girlfriends from the period would find it fitting.

BASTARD: 1986/87

I BROUGHT KATE home to Sarnia for a visit in the summer of 1986, and broke up with her there. We had been having some problems, all mine and all imaginary. But, I wanted out. She asked me twice if I wanted to break up in a 24-hour period, and the second time I was afraid she'd never ask again, so I said yes. She took it badly, big surprise, and headed straight for the train station and back to Toronto. I moved out of our apartment a few weeks later and went on the road. What a relief to have a job where you could just screw off for a few weeks when things were bad at home. I remember when Wayne Turmel got engaged, we were talking and I asked him why would he want to get married.

"Because I love her," he said.

"That's all well and good," I replied, "But once you're married, you can't just hop into the car and go off on an eight-week road trip anymore." Wayne married, divorced, went to Los Angeles, married again, had a child, and got out of the business. He became a successful corporate trainer.

While I was on my getaway road trip, my brother Richard found me a great apartment. It was the second floor of an old house a few subway stops east of Yonge and Bloor, off Pape Avenue. It was the sixth and last place I lived in Toronto. And it was my favourite. I became friends with the girl who lived downstairs. I had my old Heintzman piano. I had a restaurant a half-block away, and I could park my car in my own driveway. It was heaven. The restaurant was a Greek place and I became familiar enough to the waitress that all I had to do was walk in, sit down, and nod to her and she'd bring me what I always ordered. Two grilled cheese and a coke. Things like that always made me happy.

What wasn't making me happy in the latter part of 1986 was showcasing. As Evening At The Improv and Caroline's Comedy Hour geared up on A&E, producers began to trek to Toronto to see us Canadians. All through 1986 I showcased and bombed and didn't get it. Showcased and bombed and didn't get it. It was a broken record, and monumentally frustrating. I was doing great shows in town and on the road, killing everywhere. I could usually handle any kind of pressure show, but the mystical 'showcase' eluded me. Another problem was the regular showcase host. He was a comedian with whom I'd had several run-ins. We had never really clicked and he was pretty sure I was gay, which probably offended or perhaps even frightened him. We insulted each other constantly, face to face and behind each other's back. We loved finding weakness in the other. He, unfortunately for me, hosted a bunch of showcases in a row, always making sure I went up first. His introduction for me said it all.

"What can I tell you about your first act? I could tell you he's *a gigantic hunk of steaming shit,* but I won't. He's your first act. John Wing." Add to that intro that m'learned friend, the host, often wasn't very funny and I would come out to a cold crowd. And then forget all those silly excuses and say it was my fault. I got spooked by the showcase fever and couldn't have done a good set anywhere.

The host had an opening line that showed what his limitations were. It went something like *I'd just like to say that I'm socially well-adjusted, I love my parents, and I had a great time in school, so we have nothing to talk about, goodnight.* And he would do a fake walk-off. Not a bad idea for a joke, if a little inside. The problem was that it never got a laugh. And I mean *never*. It got a titter or two, a half-hearted chuckle at best. So, at the first big showcase in the summer of 1986, he opened with that joke. he'd probably been doing it for a year by then, And it bombed, as always. I finally clued in, watching him that night, that he was unaware that the joke didn't work. To him it was funny, so whether the audience laughed or not was immaterial. He couldn't hear them. Now, we all have jokes we think are great that never work. But you don't open a showcase with something that never works, whether you can hear it or not.

Many years later, after I'd gotten sober and my act had changed a good deal, a club owner sat me down and made me watch the video of my set the previous evening. I tried to get out of the room more than once, but she wouldn't let me leave. I tried to get out because I was horrible. Truly pathetic. I had come to that place, that affliction I had so often noticed in other performers. I wasn't getting laughs and *I didn't even know it.* Another great thing about the ever-changing job. Always lessons to re-learn. I wrote a joke once that I thought was very funny (the audience thought I was wrong) that went, *Fool me once, shame on you. Fool me twice, shame on me. Fool me three times.....aw, shit!* I still like it. It's in the Never-Worked file with *I turned thirty and was feeling pretty down about it, until I remembered that when Jesus was my age, he was still doing weddings.*

JOHN WING Jr.

BASTARD: I had come to that place, that affliction I had so often noticed in other performers. I wasn't getting laughs and I didn't even know it.

Perhaps 10 years after my run-ins with the host of the showcases, I was back in Toronto playing Yuk Yuks Uptown and he happened to be hosting. The first night, he came over and asked what I wanted him to say about me in the intro. I said whatever he wanted was fine, as long as he didn't mention that I was a gigantic hunk of steaming shit. He looked at me quizzically and asked, "Why would I say that?" He didn't recall the line.

DURING MY eight months living with Kate, I had a short affair with a Yuk Yuks waitress/actress I met while Kate was out of town. After Kate and I split, I resumed the relationship, and from the late summer until the early winter of 1986, we dated. Or, more to the point, we slept together when I was in town, which, as always, wasn't often. I'm not going to say her name, because she's more famous than I am now. Let's call her Sandra.

That fall, my car broke down for the first time, and for the last six months or so that I owned it, it broke down a lot. Once, in Detroit, I had to get an advance from the club early in the day to pay for a new radiator. I picked the car up in the early afternoon, and on the spur of the moment, decided to do a cemetery trip. There was a big one not far away, called Mount Elliot. I went and looked around a bit, but the caretaker's office was closed and it was too large to just go traipsing around, so I headed back. Upon leaving the grounds, I noticed another red light on the dash panel. In the morning it had been the temperature light. Now it was the alternator. I drove to a nearby gas station, where I was informed that another hundred-odd dollars, cash, would be required. I phoned Steve Iott at the hotel, and he drove out and lent me the money, although not without informing me what a *moron* I was for being in that neighbourhood. It was apparently a seedy, crime ridden part of town. I said I had come to see a graveyard, not a neighbourhood, to which he replied that I might end up in that goddamn graveyard if I wasn't more careful. Having disposed of his money and advice, Steve hopped into his white station wagon and left me there to fend for myself. The car was fixed and I waited for the next time, hoping against hope it wouldn't be at eighty miles an hour.

The Pontiac took a fair bit of punishment. In the almost two years I owned it, I averaged 180 kilometers a day. I was also not immune to flights of idiotic forgetfulness. Once I was late for a Yoder gig, and lost, so I pulled into a service station, hopped out and asked for directions. While the guy was showing me where I needed to go, he glanced out the window and said, "Jesus, look at that." I looked and my car was rolling down the driveway of the station, backwards, into the street, which was choked with traffic. I had forgotten to put it in park. I watched, helpless, as it barged into the late afternoon traffic and was only nicked. I ran out and saved it before it got clobbered. Another time I was driving home from Jackson, Michigan, along I-94, very late at night. I was trying to pass a truck, doing almost 80 as I pulled up next to the giant semi, when a deer decided to come across the highway from the truck's side. I saw it coming and hoped it would get across safely, but there wasn't anything I could do. If I swerved or braked I would no doubt lose control and be killed. My father's advice flashed momentarily through my head: *Always better to kill the animal rather than yourself.* He was usually talking about dogs, of course. I held my spot, slowing just a bit, but the doe didn't have the speed to beat me. I hit her in the back flank with my bad headlight, opening her up and flipping her into the ditch. I didn't stop until a few miles later, figuring it might be a good thing to relax and get my heart rate back to normal. If I'd struck her broadside, I probably would have been killed. When I got to Sarnia and stopped for breakfast with my parents, I found fur in the front grille. My father asked if I'd kept the deer.

"Why would I want to keep it?"

"You're allowed to if you kill 'em accidentally."

"I didn't know that."

"Too bad. Good meat." I wondered what I'd say to the Canadian customs official coming into Sarnia with a dead deer on the hood of the car. "Nothing to declare, thank you." Once my father had been asked at the Canadian border if he had anything to declare, and legend has it he said, "Only my utter *contempt* for the United States of America."

I was very lucky at least 50 times in that car. I was, by now, a full-fledged drug addict. I smoked pot every day, usually around noon, and again perhaps at four. Not during the show, though that was a useless dodge, since I was stoned almost every waking hour. I even used marijuana to stay awake during long night drives. If I felt myself getting tired, my eyes drifting, I would pull out a joint and smoke the first third of it. not holding the smoke in trying to get high, but just a few quick, cigarette-style puffs. Then I'd put it out. I wouldn't get high, exactly. It'd just sort of smooth out the fatigue. It would last usually around two hours, and then I'd pull out the joint and repeat the process. If it sounds foolish to the reader, imagine how it feels to write about what a complete idiot you were.

I loved getting stoned after the show. I was not a social user. Social is not a word anyone has *ever* used to describe me. I liked to get back to my room alone, get high, and watch TV. Sleep was impossible after the show. The set would run through my head. The jokes that didn't go would bug me and bug me, and the dope was a mechanism that actually slowed that dreary process, and seemed to free my mind to think of other things, or at the very least to enjoy bad, late-night television. If I was seen getting high in a group back then, it always meant that my personal supply was low or nonexistent. I had a regular guy in Toronto who was very reliable, and I got to know the ropes of buying on the road. The kitchen of the comedy club was the best place. A veritable hotbed of druggies, usually. This would often lead to wee hours car trips to condemned houses in desperate parts of town, but, luckily for me, not too many.

I even figured out a way to get marijuana through security checks at airports, and, *very* occasionally, across customs. I was obsessive and meticulous, and I had a lot of free time during the day. I would strain my buds until the whole quarter ounce was a fine, flakey powder. Then I would place the powder in the centre of a large piece of foolscap. I would tamp it down as best I could and then fold the paper over it until the dope was encased in a small square. Then I would seal the edges of the square with duct tape, and place it in my wallet at least forty-eight hours before a trip. The two days in my wallet would flatten the paper even further. I had been searched a few times, and I had noticed that they never searched my wallet. Sometimes when I was showing I.D. in the customs office, I would open the wallet and let it sit on the counter while I was questioned and/or searched. They never looked in it. The technique worked only if there were no drug sniffing dogs. Once they became widespread, I was doomed. But by then I had stopped using. Lucky lucky lucky.

One of the strangest border crossings I ever made was at Fort Erie, coming back from Rochester, one night in 1986. Coming into Buffalo was normally a cinch.

"Where're you going?"

"Buffalo."

"Where're you coming from?"

"Fort Erie."

"Are you carrying a gun?"

"No."

"Well take this. You'll need it to get through downtown." Getting back into Canada wasn't always a cinch. And I had two problems in the car with me that night. Al & George. It was Super Bowl weekend. I had a case of cheap American beer in my trunk that I was going to try and smuggle across for my Super Bowl party later that day. Al and George were both roaring drunk. Getting everyone across was going to be really hard. We stopped at a Burger King along the highway around 3 a.m. While I got food, Al and George disappeared. After a few minutes, I located them walking in the parking lot.

"Let's go, guys."

"We can't leave yet," said Al, pissed to the gills.

"Why not?" I asked.

"There's a trucker from Georgia here and he's going to show us his GUN!"

I frogmarched the boys back to the car and took off, angry with

Al. He was always up for something outrageous when he was blasted. I actually thought I was better than them because I only smoked pot, and I never let it interfere with my work (yeah, *right*). A couple of miles from the border I noticed that both my companions were unconscious. I had to stop a mile from the customs booth and shake/slap them awake. I sternly ordered that they say nothing to the customs guy unless they were asked, and to be as monosyllabic as possible. I didn't mention the beer in my trunk, for one reason because they were so addled they might have slipped and mentioned it, and for another that they might drink it all before we got back to Toronto.

After a while, my reticence to hang out on the road became well known. I once did a western tour that lasted four weeks and I did almost every gig with a guy named Tom. He wasn't somebody you trusted. He was the kind of guy who would rent a TV set from Granada and then sell it. The word was he had left British Columbia owing a shitload of money to a truckload of guys. He was a mooch and a generally slimy individual. And I could not shake him. Every night he was knocking at my hotel room door and smoking my dope. I stopped going to my room after the show because I knew he'd appear. He even got the seat next to me on the plane home. We walked to baggage claim and our bags came out at the same time! We walked together out to the taxi stand at Pearson, and he gave me a look.

"You wanna share a taxi into town?" he asked.

"No," I said, not even looking at him. I turned to the dispatcher and said, "Limo, please." A black Lincoln town car pulled up, my bags were deposited in it's giant trunk, and I was relaxing in the plush back seat in no time. As we pulled away, I put the window down and waved. *Bastard.*

Not that I was the worst bastard on the circuit. There was a guy out west who was thought to be in his own league. He picked up a young comedian for a gig once, and, wanting to dispel any ugly rumours the kid might have heard, he offered a suggestion.

"Look, I'm sure you've heard a lot about me. Some of it might be true and some of it might not, but if you want to know something, just ask me. I have no problem if you just ask me."

"Okay," said the kid, "is it true you once kicked a pregnant woman in the stomach?"

"Now this is *exactly* the kind of thing I'm talking about," said the guy. "She was not pregnant. She was just *fat.*"

Around 1986, a kid named Lou Eisen started working the circuit, first as a host. He was a sour, bitter, sharp-witted guy, and I really liked him. He was a lot like me. Grouchy and egotistical. He had trouble figuring out his stage persona at first, but he was quick and had real talent. His only real fault, to my mind, was that he whined about everything. One day I just couldn't take anymore of his moaning, so I sat him down and told him how it was.

"Look," I said, "there are three rules you need to know. One: The room sucks. Two: The food sucks. And three: You're not gonna get paid as much as you think. Now, for Christ's sake, you *picked* this fucking career. Stop bitching."

Lou reminded me of this episode several years later, after I'd been sober a few years. I could find no recollection of it at all, but he assured me that it happened. I bemoaned what a prick I must have been.

"Of course you were a prick," Lou said. "Why do you think nobody liked you?"

When I was in Florida the first time, in 1983, John Caponera came over to me one night as I was about to go on. He must have noticed that I was nervous. I thought he was going to reassure me. But he didn't.

"Listen, they don't look like your crowd, so if you want to cut it short, I'll fill your time." I bombed that show, but I never forgot the little trick, and I played it on many a young hopeful later on. Another little practical joke I learned in Florida was the "Bad Gig Story" joke. One night I was in the condo in Sarasota with Al April, Jerry Elliot, and James Wesley Jackson. You may find this hard to believe, but we were all getting high. I was asking about gigs and James said that Jerry had done a particular gig I'd heard about.

"How was that job?" Al asked Jerry.

"Oh man," Jerry replied, "it was horrible. Right from the start. I get into the airport and they've got a limo waiting for me. The owner's come to meet me. I couldn't believe it. But as soon as I got into the limo, I see there are three other guys in there waiting for me. All in biker leathers. They strip me, and rape me, fuckin' *rape* me! They all took turns fucking me in the ass the whole way in to the hotel."

I thought Jerry *might* be joking, but I was high, and I'm fairly gullible anyway. Then Al raised his head from the bong and asked, "How's the money?"

I suppose it was a form of initiation. A welcoming. I choose to believe that's what it was.

So, where was I? Oh, yes, I was dating Sandra. We'd been going along fairly well up until New Year's, 1986/87. I was in Winnipeg. Sandra had just started to complain about my being away most of December, but I wasn't worried. then she called me on New Year's Eve in Winnipeg and told me she was pregnant. Then I started to worry. But I needn't have. My reputation for being a bastard was about to become stronger than ever.

At 27, I was of course more mature than I was when I arrived in Toronto at age 20. Which means that at 20, I must have been a stone-pure idiot. I started keeping a daily journal in late December 1986 and kept it up until late September of 1987. The only other real diary I ever attempted was a summer journal when I was 11. I had fallen in love with a girl the previous school year and at the end of that year, she moved to Toronto. I spent the entire summer mooning over her, and mentioned her name in every single journal entry that summer. When I was re-reading these journals of 1987, I wasn't pleasantly surprised to discover that I hadn't changed much in the intervening 17 years. I got laid a lot more and I knew how to hurt people. Other than that, I was still 11.

JOURNAL EXCERPTS: 1987

31 Dec. 1986 Toronto

Last day of the old year. Al and George and I boarded the flight to Winnipeg at 9 a.m. We all looked in various stages of terminal illness. In December I spent a grand total of three days in my apartment and somehow I just keep going. City to city; stage to stage.

I've always hated New Year's Eve for a variety of reasons. Mostly because I always feel lonely and there's never anything good on TV. This year, I'll be with Al and George and Ron Rubin – all champion drinkers. With luck they won't stumble in and pass out until I've already done so.

1 Jan. 1987 Winnipeg

A strange New Year's. 220 people crammed into the room, and by the time I got on it was 11:15 so the last half of the show was just soldiering through while people talked loudly and horns sounded the impending numerical memory change. Performers never have any fun on this night. Going back to the dressing room I was jostled by someone and I fell against a chair, punching a small hole in the bottom of the guitar. This unnerved me so I packed up and went straight home. Watched some TV and read and went to sleep around two. Whoopee.

Bitterly cold here. Sandra called this afternoon, desperately depressed about being alone on New Year's. We resolved nothing, as usual. I long ago realized the futility of discussing how often I'm away so I clammed up and she got tearful. Maybe I should be alone forever. She was playing word games, telling me she hated walking home alone, so & so made a pass at her, etc. I wanted to watch Barry Steiger on TV but I missed it. Ahh well. Read and slept.

Fri. 2 Jan. 1987 Winnipeg

Moved into a hotel today and phoned Sandra. Then the penny dropped. She thinks she may be with child. Not only that but she's known of the possibility for over a month and not told me. No wonder she's depressed. God, I can't believe her sometimes. I am, I admit, a generally distant, distracted person but regardless, she should have informed me. Apparently her urine test was negative and tomorrow we'll get a blood test confirming it one way or the other. My anger is omni-directional and impotent right now. I don't know. I don't know anything anymore. I'm going to work now.

Someday I'll understand why I ignore and mistreat most of my girlfriends until they leave me, or if they refuse, I leave them,. When I was romantic they stepped on me or they didn't understand, or I was ignorant. So I eventually became ruthless. Ruthless John gets more girls, but it's still just a game and more and more it's harder to play.

Sat. 3 Jan. 1987 Winnipeg

Slept late and Sandra didn't call. So I called her and we broke up. Probably for the best – who knows? Maybe I am a bastard, as Jeremy says. If it be so, it were a grievous fault. I am ambitious. I want to be more famous than my mentor, Professor Caspar Milburn Duckblind. Born of dirt-poor farmers Elwood and Bertha Duckblind, Caspar had to scrabble like a wounded badger for every scholarship and accolade, but he never faltered from course until he was a widely revered playwright, poet, philosopher, lover, and professor of Comparative Do-Hickeys at the university of Slang. Then he lost it all in a frenzied, 36-hour gambling, boozing and fucking spree. When asked, at the end if his life, art and reputation were worth a day and a half of debauchery, he replied, "Perhaps." A man like this commands respect.

I don't feel loneliness much, although I spend the majority of my time alone. I do what I want when I want and who cares if I'm alone. Dealing with my own life (ego) has always been trouble enough. No more girlfriends. No more pregnancy scares. No more.

Sun. 4 Jan 1987 Winnipeg

I'm writing a film about a scientist whose laser experiment backfires and turns him into a giant zipper. I'm calling it THE FLY.

Mon. 5 Jan. 1987 En Route

We are 75 minutes from landing in Toronto and a new life. Threw away my hash and will try to go drug free for a while. Must try and write some new things. Funny, when the plane's in the air, it never seems like it's moving. I've got to find Sandra's stuff and pack it in the bag she lent me and drop it all of at her place. How we will manage this week is anyone's guess.

Since Judy – Farah, Lisa, Shelly, Karen, Kate, and Sandra. Too many women. Too much trouble. I've learned all the tricks of the so-called relationship but none of the desires. My view of time spent is decidedly Victorian, and I must stop considering it all just a game.

I didn't do a poor show last weekend, but the worst one got reviewed (usual) and he raved about me (unusual). A little dinner, perhaps some tax sorting out for an hour or so and then a quiet beginning to my headlining-at-home week. It should be interesting, since several of the upper rung of comics are mulling over another strike. Should mean some good gigs for me. I wonder if other comedians realize that one must never linger over a fallen comrade, but step up sprightly and say, "I can do that gig." The law of survival. Or, as my mother fondly puts it, "It's a jungle out there." We are now 30 minutes from arrival. I am almost.

In The Wee Hours. 6 Jan. 1987 Toronto

Got home and dropped off my things. Packed a bag with Sandra's stuff and dropped it off at her place. I just left it on her doorstep. Callous and cowardly, I suppose. She called later and told me I simply had to come over and discuss it with her. So I did. She was angry with me and at first refused to reveal the results of the test, but finally she relented and admitted she wasn't pregnant after all. Phew! I confirmed our breakup. I don't want a relationship anymore. This experience has scared me enough to keep me relatively pure for a few years. The key word is "relatively". Tomorrow's another day.

Thurs. 8 Jan. 1987 Toronto

Sandra and I are now officially broken up, and although I feel heavy guilt and a strange sadness, I know it's for the best. I have neither the guts or the inclination to love someone I never see because I love my job more. It took several harrowing days, but such are the vicissitudes. Last night, Sandra came to the show and we came back here afterward. I guess I was just trying to better explain my position. No matter what, when I'm instigating a separation, I always manage to look like a fool. She got very angry and stormed out about three a.m. I watched her stand at the corner and search for a cab. After a few minutes, she came back slowly and cried on my shoulder and then on my bed for a while. This morning I drove her home and thus our nine-month affair ended. A painful ending. As if there's any other kind.

Maybe tonight I'll be funnier.

Fri. 9 Jan. 1987 Toronto

Good show last night. Went up and smoked 'em. Sandra phoned afterward, and it alternated between about average and horribly painful. She says all I'm doing is running away and I'll end up empty and stupid. Robert Frost said, "And I may return/if dissatisfied/with what I learn/from having died. He was probably a comic.

I started a joke.....

Sat. 10 Jan. 1987 Toronto

A bizarre day. I awoke and went downtown to get my typewriter fixed and my video copied. The guy at VTR said they couldn't copy it because of the speed at which it had been recorded. It was an omen, beyond doubt. Did an audition for Adderly, and came home to prep for the show. It was a typical weekend show. Howard Nemetz hosted with Ron Vaudry and Mike MacDonald opening up. The second show was Steve Fromstein hosting and Howard replacing Ron as the opener. I had to go short first show because Mike, Ron, and Howard all did really long sets. Fuckers. I cut a lot of bits short, and was ignorant enough to forget my capo, so I spent the whole guitar set transposing in my head. The whole set was disjointed. I remembered to do feedback for Jimi Hendrix and that seemed to make it funnier. Ron was in a foul mood and I suspect that he is the leader of the so-called mutiny that appears to be in the offing. His bitterness and poor attitude have long since soured any chance of him getting anywhere within the hierarchy. He is vocal in his condemnation of Yuks management and how they fuck us. As a result, he gets fucked the most. The obvious pattern here seems to elude him as well. He's like the guy on the slave wheel who keeps turning to his blind companion and saying, "You know what? This sucks!"

Sandra asked for a ride home after the second show, and I obliged, refusing to go inside. I've broken up with her four or five times now, and surely that should be enough. I decided to go home by taking Gerrard over to Broadview and it may have saved my life. I was coming to the intersection of River and Gerrard when I went over a pothole and the rear axle snapped clean off and sent the back wheels off their moorings. It felt like the back of the car just fell off. I was doing about 40 klicks and went into a major skid, careening across the opposite lanes of traffic, there fortunately being none at that hour, and into a gas station. I managed to get the car stopped before I took out the pumps and exploded in a Bullitt-like fireball. I got out and surveyed the damage. The back axle and wheels were at a 45 degree angle to the rest of the car. It looked weird. I walked three blocks to a phone booth and called a tow. The guy showed in about a half hour. A half-hour of people and cabs driving by slowly, mouths agape. Two cops stopped for a moment, and I told them what happened. One of them snickered. I hate cops. They were probably just making sure I wasn't drunk or stoned. I wasn't. I had been on my way to get stoned when it happened, although I don't think I mentioned that.

The tow guy was a good fellow, and we got the axle back in place, sort of, and towed the beast to his garage, dropping me at home first. He saw my guitar and asked what I did.

"I'm a stand-up comic," I said.

"Really?" he asked. (They all say that.) "You're the second famous person I've towed." Turned out Donald Sutherland was his hymen-breaking famous tow.

When I finally got home I called Sandra, knowing she'd be pleased to note any misfortune on this week where she's been treated so shabbily. Ah, well. Christ had his bad days, too. I must thank him and His Father, God by name, for looking out for me along the road of life tonight. If I'd been on Bayview or the Don Valley, I'd probably be dead. *The lads who die in their glory will never be old.....*

Sun. 11 Jan. 1987 Toronto

Norm MacDonald came to the show last night. He quit smoking, the bastard. My mother has been simply fanatical of late in her quest for the health of my lungs. Over Christmas she told me that all the neighbours were depressed because I smoke so much. Having a mother is sometimes fun. Meanwhile my car sits alone in some garage in the north end. It snowed a ton last night and today. Great big wet flakes. Good packing snow.

Lorne Elliot came to the second show last night. He'd done a party at the Four Seasons and dropped in and stayed for my set. He was very complimentary afterward, and I went back to his hotel where we jammed for a couple of hours and smoked a whole bunch of his terrible dope. So much for going drug free. Today was slower. Everything is weird when you have no car. I guess I'll nap now, or clean the bathroom, or something.

Tues. 13 Jan. 1987 Toronto

After a morning of mechanics and insurance people and a new tow to my regular garage, I was so frazzled that when I showed up at my photographer's studio to have my new photos taken, he said I looked so bad we should call it off and do it next week. We got high instead. Got my typewriter back and was trying to use it when Liz called from Yuk Yuks and asked me to go to Sudbury in two hours. If I had my car, I would have done it, but I said no. She was frantic, as usual, saying no one else could do it, she'd called everybody, etc. I suggested Roger Chandler, and that calmed her down right away. So Roger ended up doing it. I love doing Liz's job. Tomorrow I have a meeting with her to set up the next few months of work. Fingers crossed.

My car insurance apparently has a loss-of-use clause. I get 25 bucks a day toward a rental car if I need it. For 25 bucks in this town, you can rent a skateboard for an hour.

Wed. 14 Jan. 1987 Toronto

I invited Elvira Kurt over for some TV watching but she begged off. I hope she doesn't think I'm only trying to fuck her. She's going to be really funny, she is, and I'm just anxious to get on the bandwagon. I am interested in fucking her, of course, but it's not a priority or anything. I suppose I really shouldn't search for a companion at Yuk Yuks, but then again where the hell else do I go every night? My heart yearns occasionally for Susan L— (514-482-9225), and that wintry Winnipeg weekend of two years ago. Never was it so simple or so sexually and intellectually satisfying.

I went to the club hoping not to run into Sandra, but of course she was there, and after some amiable chatting she started to tell me what an idiot I am for leaving her. Since I'd now had a few days alone, why didn't I just come back to her? Christ, just like high school only she's playing my part. Went home depressed.

Thurs. 15 Jan. 1987 Toronto.

A long day. I woke up late and tried, unsuccessfully, to raise the mechanic and the appraiser of my car. I feel utterly powerless without it. I've already turned down $750 worth of work because I don't have it. Finally the guy called and the insurance will pay some, but not all of the cost, I'll have to kick in $415, which is not bad, considering. At least we have a decision. Now all I need to know is how long until I get it back? The said to call him tomorrow on that. Tomorrow and tomorrow...

Elvira Kurt called out of the blue. Well, perhaps not entirely out of the blue. We had a nice conversation and she offered to drive me to

253

Belleville on Monday. I'll believe it later, if they force me. I got two verses and two choruses of a song finished, and I would term it mildly funny. But it's a start. Liz called as I was stripping to bathe and offered me yet another gig I had to turn down. Naked, no less. Shit. Sometimes the snake around my neck constricts so much I can hardly breathe, but to cut it away would merely slit my throat. La Chaim Potok.

Fri. 16 Jan. 1987 Toronto.

Another day of riveting inactivity. I probably won't get my car back until after the Super Bowl. I find it strange how impotent I feel without it. At least the problem is solved and the costs allocated. And I'm booked up till May the tenth. One hundred and ten days ahead. Forty-nine days here, and sixty-one days away.

I called Elvira and we're definitely going to Vermont on Tuesday. So it's Belleville on Monday and Vermont on Tuesday.

Wrote a few jokes today and cleaned. Mom and Dad are coming.

Sat. 17 Jan. 1987 Toronto

Went to Yuk Yuks Studio on Queen Street and watched Elvira perform. I was surprised. She seems to have culled Bruce McCulloch's style of performing. She is physical in an abstract way and glides from one side of the stage to the other, just like Bruce does. Her jokes are good – some of them. She could edit her act better, but so could almost everyone. Even me, I must shamefully admit. We talked afterward and she seemed excited about our upcoming driving adventure. I can't tell if she really likes me yet. I'm sure she can see my intentions engraved in marble. She plays it very cruel, I mean cool. I guess you could call that one a Jungian slip. Karl's on his ass over that slip.

I was about to leave the Studio when Jane, a Yuks waitress, Ron Vaudry's girl, and Sandra's friend rolled into one screwed-up babe, called me aside and asked me why I was being such a bastard to Sandra. I said I was sparing her the incredible pain of finding out just how much of a bastard I really am. Then I cut her short, since it really isn't any of her damn business. She should talk. Once when she was pissed at Ron she set fire to his car.

Leaving the Studio finally, I cabbed it up to the Tarragon theatre to meet mom and dad and see my sister Paula in a play. Allegra F—— was there, a ravishing actress friend of Paula's. We made small talk, and I tried to ask her out for tomorrow night but made a poor job of it. We parted wondering. If I go out with her, I'll have to miss the third period of the Leaf-Oiler game. Is any woman worth such sacrifice? I like Allegra, and she'd undoubtedly be a great-to-middling fuck. She'd be great. I'd be middling. Wait a minute, I don't middle. I headline. We'll see, rabbit, we'll see.

Sun. 18 Jan. 1987 Toronto

Call me Ishmael. All my whaling buddies call me Ishmael. I watched the first half of the Leaf-Oiler game, gave my boots a polish, and headed over to the Tarragon. I ended up with Paula and Allegra and a big group of actors. The seating left me far from Allegra and no chance at private conversation. Although I did raise her ire when I said that art and politics don't mix. She lashed out at me, saying that being political is the duty of every artist. Horseshit. Allegra is really pretty. She seems sharp and independent as well. She's my age, and if

255

I go after her I must be out of my mind.

Today, I actually phoned Susan L—. We haven't seen each other for two years, but I got her number from the Montreal operator and I called, feeling very foolish. Her artiste boyfriend answered and was instantly suspicious. I gave my name and Susan and I had a strange but true conversation. Once she confirmed to him that I was indeed an old flame, the jealous bastard turned the stereo up to 11 and started shouting at her. I apologized and we rang off. I don't know whether or not I should have done it. (Yes I do) Somehow it all helps, though. I've got to get out of this rut. I'll go do my laundry and come home and pack my bag. Something big is coming. I can feel it.

Thurs. 22 Jan. 1987 Ottawa

A fascinating few days. Elvira couldn't go to Belleville, and I was going to go with B.J. Woodbury, but the weather was so bad that I had them stop at the last subway stop north and let me off. I declined to risk my life in the blizzard conditions for a Belleville show. First time I've ever done that. Then on Tuesday Elvira and I drove to Burlington, Vermont to do a show there. She was fabulous, as always. Keen conversation and the discovery of many shared viewpoints and experiences. She did a great show, warming the audience up so I could boil them. Then we drove all the way back to Ottawa. It was an eleven-hours-in-the-car day. We shared my room at the Beacon Arms, and fell asleep holding each other. There was some kissing, a fair bit of tongue, but no intercourse. It was really a fun day (and night). Elvira went back to Toronto on Wednesday, so I could have some quiet time to obsess about her.

Last night Sandra called late, really pissed off because she'd found out about the waitress at the uptown club I slept with last fall. Luckily the conversation was brief.

"Can I ask you one question?"

"Of course."

"Did you sleep with that waitress uptown while we were seeing each other?"

"Not while we were seeing each other, no."

"But you slept with her in September, didn't you?"

"That's two questions," I said, and hung up. Yeah I slept with a damn waitress from Uptown. Jesus. Who fucking cares now? She came up to me and said she thought I was attractive and I was tempted, since in 27 years it's the only time it's ever happened, so we went to her place and had sex, and halfway through it, her boyfriend came to the door. She went to the door naked and somehow managed to blow him off, which took a while, and get back to blowing me off, which took a while longer.

Two shows tonight. I hope I'm up for them.

Fri. 23 Jan. 1987 Ottawa

I called Elvira and we chatted amiably. But I don't want to read too much into it. She's great and there are a lot of good signs. And I can't tell anyone about it. Just what I've always wanted.

I was better on the first show tonight. All guitar. I wrote a new song but I was too scared to do it. Of course. Howie doesn't like my dog with no legs bit, and I feel his critique should be noted here. It has been so noted.

My favourite gifts are the ones that you give back when you break up. Is that funny?

Maybe it should be 'get' back when you break up. Keep trying.

Mon. 26 Jan. 1987 Toronto

Elvira came over and watched the Super Bowl, which was half a good game. When it was over, I thought she might stay around for something physical, but she called someone and made plans. Then we wrestled for a little while. She says she thinks having sex with me would be fun. But not on Super Sunday, apparently. We really talk and truly like each other, but the game rituals must be observed. Building confidence and trust. Making her believe that fucking isn't *all* to you. you're not *always* anxious to fuck. You like the simpler, tender, with-the-clothes-on moves. You promote friendship over Biblical toad-sexing. We have slept together, but it was a superficial and circumstantial coupling. If we'd had sex that night, it would have been a *fantastic* superficial and circumstantial coupling.

There you have it for the first month of my most important year. The show was really going well, so I wasn't as focused on it. I was out chasing pussy. "No more girlfriends." Yeah, right. Got rid of one troublesome woman and moved on to attempt three more. Luckily, I really was too damn busy. And something else happened around that time. Joan Rivers left the Tonight show and signed with Fox to do her own show. It probably wouldn't have made a lot of difference except that she hired Mark Breslin to book comedians for the show. In a showcase a few weeks after the last entry, I finally killed and got hired for George Schlatter's Comedy All-Stars in Los Angeles. Everything I dreamed of was getting closer, so it was hard to concentrate on getting laid. However, I managed it.

Everything in my career happened after I thought it should. Usually long after. When I was sure I was ready for some move up, some accolade, or some television show, meant that it would be one to two years before I was actually ready. Being really ready meant that there was only one chance in five hundred that I'd screw it up. Unlike any other kind of performing, TV is really standing on the precipice, telling yourself not to look down. Richard Lewis bombed on his first Tonight Show and didn't get back on for at least 10 years. Jackie Mason supposedly gave Ed Sullivan the finger and didn't appear on television for 20 years. Two really funny guys who made little mistakes that had far reaching consequences. Andy Kindler had a character he used to do in his act, a bad and bitter comedian who tells tales of being canceled. "They canceled the fuckin' week on me!" One of his stories was about a Tonight Show shot. "...finally I get my Tonight Show shot, finally, and I'm backstage, reminding myself, 'Don't say pussy, say vagina. Don't say pussy, say vagina'. I get out there, I say 'cunt', I'm off network FIVE YEARS! You say 'cunt' on cable you're a big star!" It was fictitious, but we all knew the possibility was there.

TV SHOWS: 1987

W HEN JOAN RIVERS hired Mark, I came up with a plan. Mark had promised me a few things over the years, and I don't think any of them had ever panned out. But I never expected they would. That was the deal. When something is *promised*, it's almost surely not going to happen. That's more the essence of showbiz than anything else. *Hurry up and wait. You got it. You don't have it. They promised. It's all off. They say next month...* And you'd better get used to it. I had always liked Mark, even if I didn't trust him in all matters. He read poetry as well as novels, which was rare among comedic types. He could converse on any subject except sports, which bored him silly. Most comedians talked about sports, dope, fucking, and TV, period. Mark was, and is, a really, really smart guy. I knew he would see my plan for what it was, but I also knew he would appreciate the gesture. I asked him out to lunch.

We went to a place on Yorkville Street near where he lived, and I got right to the point.

"Listen," I said, "when you make up your list of Canadian guys for Joan Rivers, I want to be on that list." I don't think I had ever specifically asked him for a favour before (I may be wrong about that) but I was going to make this one count. The key is never what you wish for, but wishing for it at exactly the right time. "I feel I deserve it and I'm reliable. I'll kill on the show and make you look good." He agreed that I deserved it and that I'd do well, but there were guys who deserved it more than I did, and they'd get the first shots. I'd be on the list, but he wouldn't know where for a while. I liked that.

"I don't want you to promise me anything," I said.

"Believe me," he replied, "I won't. Who knows how long I'll have the job?"

He asked if my set was ready today, saying that I might get a call and have to come immediately, so the set had to ready at a moment's notice. That one made me feel good. Though there was no way to be sure, I knew deep down that I would do the Rivers show. Mark would come through. And he did. It just took a lot longer than I expected.

I went on a long road trip out west for all of March, 1987. I spent most of it trying to get laid and hoping Elvira would call me. Or calling her machine. She had a way of never answering her phone or returning calls that drove me buggo. I probably left her a few hundred messages in the three months or so we were a going concern. The messages would always start off bright and witty, but eventually would degenerate into a hellishly bitter and desperate raving. We had a couple of get-togethers and attempted intercourse once. It didn't really go that well, since I still wasn't really good at it and she was well, *gay*. I wasn't absolutely aware of this fact while I was pursuing dear Elvira, but I doubt that the true knowledge of it would have stopped me, either. She was just such an appealing person. We still like each other a lot, and whenever we meet, which is rare now, our conversation starts right up where it left off the last time, even if the last time was five years ago.

The end of the western trip found me in Winnipeg, where three months before I'd received news of Sandra's pregnancy that wasn't. There was more news to come. We go to the journal.

Tues. 24 Mar. 1987 Winnipeg

I went to bed early last night and was just drifting off to never-never land when the phone rang. It was Sandra. She was feeling pretty blue. As it turns out she *was* pregnant, and two days ago she was in a car accident and miscarried. I find it hard to sort out my feelings. We had a marathon conversation, complete with more vitriolic bile spewing. I can't decide how I should deal with this (other than to fall on my knees). My immediate thoughts run to simple solutions. No more sex. No more women, except Elvira, for now. Since I am such a coldhearted, calculating bastard, it would appear simple enough. Poor Sandra. She claims she will never be able to trust again. I should never have gotten involved with her., but maybe this experience will make me realize my huge limitations in the area of love. I will endeavour not to test said limits again. Sandra said I'd better not do this to another girl. I don't think I will. Women are so emotional about these things. Oh, well. My child is dead and no one will ever know. She told me about it when I was here in January, and it ends when I return to Winnipeg three months later. The cycle turns. The worm rolls.

Got my hair cut today at Suzanne Querels. A good one. Bought a new jacket and a shirt. Watching TV now. May nap later.

I CAME ON to no less than three women that week and bedded one. So much for my vaunted, "no more" anthem. I was working and staying in the condo with a comedienne named Lisa, whom I'd dated a couple of years before. She had a pregnancy scare as well when we broke up, although a little in-my-head math proved that one false. She was just trying to scare me because I was leaving her. She was the one who handed me the phone in Winnipeg the night Sandra called. And just in case Alanis Morrissette is reading this; baby, *that's* ironic.

Sat. 28 Mar. 1987 Winnipeg

Last night I came home with Barb and we made love for a couple of hours. It was beautiful and I really needed it. She was, and is, gorgeous, with red hair, green eyes, and a fabulous body. We made love slowly and enjoyed every second.

Somewhere a child is born. But it is not my child. My child died in his mother's womb. Am I responsible for the death of a three-month-old foetus? No doubt I'll be on the judgement list for this one. Perhaps from now on I'll seek the path of fewer women. I'm really not much into whoring, although last night had its moments.

Joan Rivers looms in my brain. The ratings are low, and everyone says it's going for more talk and less comedy. And I don't have my date yet, although it must be soon. Almost everyone else in the group has done it. I must be next. I can taste it, I can smell it, I want this shot more than anything. More than sex. More than peace of mind. Joan Joan Joan, Joan Rivers.

Wed. 1 Apr. 1987 Toronto

Upon arriving home I secured my messages. The first was a sad one. Jane called to tell me that Sandra was in the hospital. It undoubtedly has to do with the miscarriage. Probably some internal injury

TV BECKONS: In the early days, we were all jonesing to do The Alan Hamel Show… Out of Vancouver, it was Canada's version of the afternoon talk show for most of the '80s.

from the car accident. I hope she's all right and I'll go see her tomorrow. Is it all my fault? Jane made it sound like it was. I made her pregnant. That couldn't have happened unless I was there. I didn't cause any of these injuries, though. God, if this doesn't convince me that I'm a bastard and should stay away from women, what will it take? or not. Maybe I'm a nice guy and I just hide it so well. Maybe I'm a sadistic, bizarre, eccentric motherfucker. *I don't know, Ralph. maybe the phrase just fits.*

Oh, and I got the Rivers show. Got a date, anyway. Had a long talk with Mark and it should be May 18th or 19th. An eventful April first. How will I deal with the future and atone for the past? Is there going to be absolution for any of this?

Then, a sail appeared. It was the devious cruising RACHEL, who, in her search for her missing children, had found only another orphan.

Fri. 3 Apr. 1987 Toronto

Had my meeting with Connie at Yuks. We mapped out the career for the next few months. It was fun, relaxed, and businesslike at the same time. People were filling out job applications and comics were coming in and out. I saw Norm MacDonald and Scott Orloff. Scott is hosting Mississauga Sunday night. He's never played the room before. They'll eat him alive, which might be fun to watch. Chatted with Pat Bullard for a while. Everyone is asking about the Rivers Show — are you excited are you excited are you EXCITED? I can't really say I am — yet. I'm coming up to the most important part of my career and have no one to share it with. My own fault, of course.

Sat. 4 Apr. 1987 Toronto

Visited Sandra at the hospital this morning. It was depressing because she was sick and really down. Bored and lonely and still in love with me. Bad combinations. Hospitals are even hellish to visit, but the fear they bring up in me is nothing to what it must be like to stay in one. I brought her some books and a bit of good cheer. I can't understand why she still wants to see me. But then, I've never understood anything about women in general. Go west, young man. Go east, young man, just get the hell out of here.

My apartment is one giant goddamn mess, but I'm doing great shows and have plenty of money. So who cares?

Thurs. 16 Apr. 1987 Rockford, Ill.

I dream of having kids and naming them well. Such hollow fantasies fill this existence. I don't really want many things that appear to be expected of me. Will I ever marry, or will I find this traveling mistress the settled-for choice? My mail is read to me over the phone by my brother. My friends and I never see each other. My sex life is feast or famine, and we are steeped in a lack of potatoes right now. God is dead, or maybe he's just losing weight.

I bought that new toy today. The Klaus Barbie doll. Wind him up and he denies everything.

Rivers in a month. or so. Los Angeles, Forest Lawn, my career, my shows. Kill 'em. Fuck 'em up. Make them laugh so hard they forget where they are. The set is close to ready. Pregnancy joke - Stud - Glasses - 364 days - Comedy's better - I can relate - perform alone - laugh at what I say - tell jokes live 'em - wasn't big enough - 45 to an hour - worth the money - technical virgin - 87 Honda - Condoms when I'm alone - game conditions - bought some - naked - glow in the dark - shortsighted - big toe - nice day - St. Bernard - fat lady - rear wheel - heavy smoker - tractor salesman - suck on my toes.

Maybe now I can sleep.

OF COURSE, my early versions of the set were ridiculously long. A six-minute television set for someone who works as slowly as I did then is twelve jokes minimum, and 15 to 18 jokes maximum. There are 25 jokes in that version. But I had only done one TV show up to that time. In the early days, we were all jonesing to do *The Alan Hamel Show,* which later became *The Alan Thicke Show.* Or, as we liked to say, "Same show. Different Alan." Out of Vancouver, it was Canada's version of the afternoon talk show for most of the '80s. Larry Horowitz had the worst experience there. the audience was made up of what Al April used to call 'retirees parents', and they weren't always the swiftest bunch. Larry went on one afternoon and was three minutes into a mediocre set when the director stopped him and said that something had gone wrong with the tape. Larry had to *start over,* do his opening three minutes a second time for a group that didn't care for it a whole lot the first time.

Thurs. 23 Apr. 1987 Rochester, NY

Tuesday night late, Shelly phoned and we made plans for yesterday. Wednesday was a prepping-for-travel day. At 11 I found myself in a strange restaurant in the Beaches waiting for Shelly. She is a sweet, if slightly bent girl. She does some acting and is paid by her parents to go to the racetrack and bet their system. One of the more peculiar parent-child relationships I've heard about. We took a walk and felt each other up a bit in her car. I am torn about it. I really want to fuck her, but I doubt I'll want much of anything after I do fuck her. What the hell. I can't worry too much. I'm a chick magnet. And who could have predicted that?

Elvira has had her machine off for several days and the obvious solution still escapes me. I call every few hours. It isn't so much the silent rejection, but more her refusal to keep any lines of communication open. I feel like telling her to go fuck herself, in a classy way.

The crowd was fairly large for a Thursday. God knows why, but I felt rusty. Just before I went on, Mark phoned and said my customs came through so we're definitely on for May 19th. Good news. I'm beginning to get a bit nervous.

Sat. 25 Apr. 1987 Rochester

First show just over. I practiced dour-faced setups to the side, and punchlines back to the centre. It seemed to work. I think I did 42 or 43 minutes. Some changes worked. others did not work. I used Milwaukee as my pregnant waitress city, and it went very well. I changed '43 minutes better' to 40 minutes and it seemed a lot smoother. Shorter and easier to pronounce. Edited liberally to cut down the set for first show timing. Pretty good crowd. Only a couple of pockets of dead air and they were my fault.

I wrote three funny postcards to Elvira last night, but I doubt I'll send them. Her machine was still off as of three a.m., but I didn't try today. This strictly enforced separation has done its dirty work well, I suppose. Too bad. Some awfully good jokes in those postcards.

Lou Dinos did Rivers last night. I didn't see it, but Howard Lapides, the owner of the Rochester Yuk Yuks, said it was a B to a B minus. Jeremy Hotz gave me a good joke, and he said we're finally even for the one-word killer I gave him three years ago. He calls me 'bastard'. No doubt a popular nickname among my lady friends. Darling I love you but give me Park Avenue. I went to the snow shed to look for my snow shoes. There they were – *gone*.

I leased a new car that April. I got to the point where I owed $600 on the Pontiac and figured I could convince some dealer to give me that much for it. Went out to Brampton and got a burgundy 1987 Plymouth Sundance for $320 a month. In a little under two years, I had driven the car over one hundred and sixty thousand kilometers. My record was a thousand kilometers in a day, Madison, Wisconsin to Toronto.

Fri. 1 May. 1987 Toronto

Rivers in 18 days now. I saw Uncle Dirty on the show last night, going under his real name, Robert Altman. The set was fine, and if he can do well, I should kill. I must kill. I must destroy them all. Wrote a new song to try at Yuks, It may work. I think it's funny enough. I've written five or six in the last two months but none of them could really cut it onstage. My usual music, three chords and a simple bridge. Nothing fancy. It's called The Meaningless Sex Blues.

Long ago I met a girl in a bar.
She had an apartment, and I had a car.

I guess you could say it was lust at first glance.
She said, "My name's Alice." I said, "Call me Lance."

My dear may I buy you a bottle of bud?
You're a beautiful woman, and I'm such a stud.
        (I am. Fuck you. I am)
If I like your mammaries and you like my pecs,
Would you care to indulge in some meaningless sex?

Let's have some meaningless sex.
Like Catherine the Great and her wonder horse Rex,
You can name your position, concave or convex,
Oh let's have some meaningless, rip-roaring sex.

You say you like it like this, I say fine.
I'll make sure you have yours long before I have mine.
You can make promises you'll never keep.
And I'll say I love you when I'm sure you're asleep.

Oh, let's have some meaningless sex,
Oh, let's get creative with the Proctor-Silex.
And when it's over, you can yell, "Okay NEXT!"
Oh, let's have some lovely, Australian Rules sex.

And I will take Alice to Debbie Does Dallas
And hope that she won't be repelled.
Cause her breasts I adore 'em

We'll both write to 'Forum',
With our names and addresses withheld,
By request.
Let's jump in molasses right up to our asses,
Oh, let' have some meaningless, marginal, spine-tingling
Meat-packing, bloodcurdling, bone-crushing, foot-stomping sex!

The crowd at Yuks was a motley crew. Al Rae, of Al & George, was there, and thank God for it, cause he's always funny. A wafer-thin Scot with a gigantic appetite for liquor. Several months ago, a doctor told him if he continued to drink at present pace, he'd be dead in two years. He is 23 years old. He was on the wagon for a while, but now he's back to his beer. I should talk. He'll die of cirrhosis and I'll die of lung cancer. Like it matters.

My set went well, and after I got off, Al came up to me, a bit in his cups, and sang a short parody he'd thought of for the Meaningless Sex song. It began, "I have a meaningless act. It doesn't mean anything and that's a fact..." The impressive thing was that he sang it right to my face. You have to like Al. Otherwise, you'd hate him.

Gary David was the headliner. A consummate professional. He's in his mid-50s now and has been around since they were doing comedy at Starvin' Marvin's back in the early seventies with Frenchy MacFarlane and Rummy Bishop. Gary's a nice guy and, though his act is a little old school, it's also polished and very funny in spots. Tonight he said, *"I was in a bar last night that was so tough if you had two ears, you were a fag."* Gary's a nice guy, too. He takes photos of the cenotaphs in every town he plays.

There were some young punks there as well. The only one I knew was Scott Orloff. He's a stupid little jerk and his act stinks and nobody likes him. Just like me, except my meaningless act is pretty good these days. I arrived early, was cynical and insulting to almost everyone, did a blistering set and fucked off.

Mon. 4 May 1987 Toronto

Saturday I drove Frankie Cramer and Lisa-Gaye Tremblay to St. Catharines and back and we did a dynamite show. I got an encore, and best of all, Lori from the office was there to see it. A bunch of hecklers made it interesting, but I never stopped working and had a great time. The car conversation was all shoptalk and bitchery. Fun, but I have to be careful about flapping my gums. Lisa found out about Elvira and me from Steve Iott, of all people. He's friends with her former fiancee. She mentioned that, of the three working females these days, I'd slept with two of them. It's true, I've seen 'em both naked, and I plan to have it off with the third one before too long. You say she's gay? That's never discouraged me. So it'll take longer and be less satisfying, so what? I'm John Wing - Comedienne-fucker. Though some would take out the 'comedienne' part.

The new car did a fairly normal 325-klick weekend. Normal for me, anyway. The Rivers countdown is at 15 days. I think about it only when I'm awake. When I'm asleep I dream about it, which isn't exactly thought.

Big comic's meeting tomorrow at Uptown. Elvira will be there. Haven't laid eyes on her since February tenth. The night she told me I was too intense. I wrote a joke about it. *My girlfriend said I was too*

273

intense, so I stared at her until she cried. Adventures loom. Life begins again and again.

Wed. 6 May 1987 Toronto.

The meeting of the fraternity took place last night at the Uptown club. Everyone was there except maybe Howard Busgang. Mark led off and went through the usual crapola. Work hard, keep plugging, keep me happy, eventually everyone will be rich and famous blah, blah, blah. Then came the business report from the head honchos, in order, Alan Gerskop, Jeff Silverman, Connie Winkleman, Ed Smeall, and Lori, of course. It was mildly amusing to watch those who are our superiors squirm a little while droning out their yearly reports. Then, in a rather surprise move, Scott Orloff was called up to testify. Scott had been unhappy with his lot of gigs at Yuks and had gone over to work for Zoe Stotland, Mark's main competitor in the college area. She's a peach, great to work for, (although I don't anymore because of the ban), but Scott being as bad as he is, she didn't have a whole lot for him, either. So he came crawling back, and in order to get his lowly spot back on the Yuks pole, he had to get up and tell us that Zoe was a liar and all her gigs are lousy rooms for shit money. None of which, of course, is true. Scott might have made it through the grovel pit unscathed if it weren't for Al Rae. Al started asking him questions like "Scott? Why are you *doing this?*" Al was drunk, naturally. And he should have kept his mouth shut. Scott was flustered, just like he often is onstage when heckled, but he managed to go with the party line one more time and was eventually rescued by Mark. A melodrama poorly acted all round.

Then Mark got up and outlined the pay raises. A 50-buck bump across the board, and a profit sharing plan that, on a weekend where every show sells out, could net a comedian perhaps $60. Whoooo eeee.

After the money had been doled out to the poor, we got around to beefs. Mark's biggest tirade was regarding the aftermath of the *Monitor* piece about unfair business practices at Yuk Yuks. He was loudly disappointed that the comedians did not rise up *en masse* and cry foul. The loyalty oath crusade revisited. How anyone could be thick enough to ask a group of comedians to act as a whole is beyond me. We all kept straight faces, being experts. The meeting finally ended around ten, and I tried to get close to Elvira but I was ignored, which drove me absolutely insane. She doesn't want any contact with me at all, apparently.

Found some great graves this morning at Mount Pleasant Cemetery. Glenn Gould, Mackenzie King (a mammoth stone), Fred Banting, and Charlie Conacher. It relaxed me no end. No end, I say.

Wed. 13 May 1987 Toronto

Haven't written for a few days. Everywhere I go people ask about the set, as though I'm not obsessing enough about it anyway. Went to the downtown club for Amateur night to practice the all important six minutes. Mike MacDonald was there, and Glen Foster, and Larry Horowitz and Howard Busgang. I went up and did the prototype. Glen timed it at six minutes and 17 seconds. Then he made a couple of excellent suggestions as to content. Mike and Buzzy sat down with me and we discussed jokes and positioning. Larry made some weird comments about making the jokes funnier, but it was nice to see the respect. They were all willing to help. Went home and rewrote it for the fortieth time. Called Elvira. I have to stop doing that.

Exactly six days from now I'll be on national television. Since the day I read the hockey speech at St. Peter's, fourteen years ago, I've wanted this. One shot at that crowd on that night. With EVERYONE watching. I wonder if my old English teacher, Mrs. Molland, will be watching. She said I wasn't funny. She gave me a B. She will pay.

Tried to lie down but the set ran through my head until I got up and worked on it some more. It still needs tweaking. Something is missing. My attention span is for shit. Probably the marijuana.

Fri. 15 May. 1987 Toronto

I'm watching Joan Rivers' last show. Dad called at 8:30 this morning to inform me that she'd been fired, the show scuttled. I received the news sleepily, and went back to bed until the radio station, CKJD Sarnia, called and wanted a comment. What could I say? I live in Toronto and it was all happening 2,500 miles away. I finally got Mark on the phone and he said it was a bloodbath. He thinks the show will go on with a new host. So I was telling everybody who called that it was probably still a go. Privately, I'm dubious, but who can tell? Went out and bought the TV Guide because my name was in it. I showed it to my waitress at the Shishkebob House where I usually eat lunch. She seemed slightly impressed.

I'm smoking way too much. This is just a test of the emergency breathing system. I tried to get Mark again but no soap. The longer it takes to reach him, the more I'll smoke. Ha ha. I'm not even half-packed. Maybe Los Angeles is just a dream.

The Joan Rivers Show continued for awhile with Arsenio Hall hosting. After two more months of tentative dates and immigration screw-ups, I finally flew down to Los Angeles on July 14th. By then I was so blasé about it, my new girlfriend thought I was a little nuts.

"How can you *not* be excited?" she kept saying. But I knew that getting excited again was death. I had waited too damn long. I had to be cool. I arrived in L.A. and was met by a limo driver and taken to my hotel in a white stretch limo, the second limousine ride I ever had. I stayed at the Hyatt Regency on Sunset Boulevard, right next to The Comedy Store. I dropped my bags in the room and went straight over to the Store. I paid $7 to get in, the first time I'd paid to get into a comedy show since 1980. I sat down at a small table in the back, and John Caponera, my old Florida colleague, was introduced. I hadn't seen him in four years. When John finished, Richard Pryor was introduced. He walked right by me on his way up there. I could *smell* him, for God's sake. He did about 20 minutes and after I hung out with John in the back parking lot. When I returned to the hotel, I met Steve Allen coming through the lobby. It was unreal.

The next day I did my first national television show. The Late Show with Arsenio Hall. My dressing room had a fruit basket and champagne. I record this fact because the majority of dressing rooms I'd been in before that rarely boasted more than a mouldy potato chip. The other guests were Elinor Donahue of *Father Knows Best,* and The Busboys. Mark walked me around the set, showing me where I'd enter and the mark I'd have to stand on. He also gave me the single best piece of advice I'd ever received about doing a big pressure show.

"Walk *slowly*," he said. He meant when I was introduced and the curtain parted. Don't rush to the mark. Walk slowly. You've got the job. Let them see you. Keep your composure.

My opening line didn't get what I'd hoped, but I quickly slipped into rhythm. A new joke I'd added just a couple of days before the show killed, and I was off, zipping through the 18 jokes that were the final version. Mark had made some excellent cuts on the afternoon of the show. My senses were so alive and I was paranoid about what I was doing with my hands, not to mention a quaking left knee, which always happened on a big set. There were bursts of applause and I could hear Arsenio and the band laughing behind me. The opera joke *(I dated a fat girl. She was really fat. I took her to the opera once and nobody would leave until she sang)* did very well, and I saw the yellow light which meant I had a minute left. I did my last three jokes pretty fast, and finished up just as the red light came on. The time had gone so slowly in my head, and so fast everywhere else. Mark was jubilant afterward, and everyone congratulated me. As I cleared out of the studio, one of the Busboys said, "Hope you get laid."

I spent three days in Los Angeles, doing another show, George Schlatter's Comedy All-Stars, and going to graveyards and bookstores. I made some contacts in the management field, and had one truckload of fun. All the time I'd lived in Toronto, I'd said I would never go to L.A., but now I'd been there, and I forgot about my promises. Now I had to find a way to get there and stay there. I consulted an immigration lawyer in Toronto, and he said the only sure way to get in was to marry an American girl. That wasn't a possibility. Yet.

Sandra and I didn't see each other again after she got out of the hospital. She eventually ended up in Los Angeles herself. I heard her on a radio commercial one night in 1997, and I got her phone number from the L.A. operator. It took a couple of days to phone her, because I was nervous. I tried to make whatever verbal amends I could for what a prick I'd been to her. She was exceedingly gracious and kind. We even met at a comedy show one night and were very friendly. She and her actor husband have been doing very well, and this past year she starred in a movie that got a good deal of press. One article, in the *Los Angeles Times*, described her in the last paragraph as 'the 32-year-old actress'. This would mean that when we dated, she was barely 16, or even younger. I could be liable for some criminal carnal charges here. I should talk though. According to my manager, I'm only 35.

For a while I had suspected that I would end up married to a comedienne. Who else could understand the lifestyle? I had dated a few of them, you will recall, with somewhat consistent results. I don't know what tipped me that this one would be different. Perhaps that she was heterosexual. That certainly helped.

DAWN: 1987/88

I WENT TO Edmonton for a Western tour in early October of 1987. I had a lovely girlfriend back in Toronto, and life was good. In Edmonton, we stayed at a condo a couple of blocks from the club. Arriving there, I found Brent Piaskoski, a young Alberta comedian, who would be opening the shows, and Dawn Greene, an Oregon girl who now lived in Los Angeles. I had barely put my luggage down when Brent suggested that Dawn and I accompany him to a lunch date with an old friend of his. I had only met Brent once, I didn't know his friend, and Dawn and I had known each other for all of two minutes, but we all went to lunch. Brent and his friend had a somewhat private conversation at lunch, so Dawn and I got talking. She was 31, five-foot-two, blond, (a real blond, she claimed, which proved to be so) sharp featured, with the palest blue eyes. And smart as a whip. We hit it off right away. All through the afternoon we talked, finding much to speak about. I liked her way too much way too soon. How she felt about me I'm not sure, and I'm not going to go ask her now. She probably thought I was a dork.

We went to the show that night and I was praying her act would be impressive. It was so hard to really like someone who had a lousy act, in my experience. Thankfully, her act was pretty good, not fabulous, but cute and clever and she was obviously a pro. I didn't dwell on what was good about it that night, however. Perhaps she hadn't clued in to how cocky I was yet, so I went right over to her when she came off.

"Do you know what your act needs?" I asked her.

"What?"

"Funnier jokes." And then I was introduced and gone to the stage, leaving her a bit open-mouthed, I'm sure. She wrote later that it wasn't the usual come-on from a headliner. I would counter that I wasn't the usual headliner. She also wrote that I'd transformed myself for the show, having shaved, combed my hair and put on my dress shirt, slacks and vest. There was a great difference then in how I looked when I wasn't working, when I'd be unshaven, almost always in a baseball cap, and generally unkempt. But I cleaned up well. As Dawn put it, "Except for the bright red glasses, he looked like he should be going door-to-door with religious pamphlets." That was the first night of our four-week trip through the prairies.

For some reason, perhaps that I may have been right, she let the opening comment about her act pass. We got to know each other a little bit that first week. Then came Calgary, where I made my move. I showed her my poetry, always a good way to get women hot, and she took my manuscript away to her room to read in private. I found out later that it frightened her. One day, we went for a long walk to a graveyard I wanted to photograph. We brought a little lunch with us and picnicked in the cemetery. That was our first date.

We had, from that first lunch in Edmonton, a mental click about each other. We were instinctive kindred spirits. Which was fine. Wonderful, even. But I wanted to fuck, which proved to be very difficult. After she read my poetry there were a couple of nights we necked and wrestled in my room after the show, but no clothes were shed, and she always stopped everything just as it was getting interesting. Then she stopped coming to my room, period.

We went to Saskatoon, staying at the Bessborough Hotel, the best hotel in western Canada, in my opinion, and while I could get her outside during the day, she was nowhere to be found at night. We walked all over Saskatoon, visiting graveyards and bookshops and the university campus, along the river. We took pictures of each other, and were, in the daylight, a young couple falling in love. But after the show I was always alone and after a week or so of this, I began to get really pissed off. So, back to Edmonton for a bunch of one-nighters, we weren't really talking anymore.

The big show that week was in Fort McMurray, a small town about 600 kilometers from Edmonton. We were given Bill Robinson's car, a giant, mid-'80s Thunderbird. Bill was the owner of the western Yuk Yuks clubs. Going up to the Fort were Brian Hartt, Dawn, and me. I did most of the driving, with Dawn spelling me for an hour or so. We got to Fort McMurray around four o'clock and found the hotel to be a pit. No TV, bad furniture, bad beds. I suggested that we drive back to Edmonton after the job, rather than stay in that pisshole. We wouldn't be getting back until five or six a.m. but, to my surprise they both agreed.

The show was tough. Brian hosted, and although he was a great writer, he hadn't spent a lot of time playing northern Alberta dives, so he didn't know what to do if the audience was, say, hostile and screaming obscenities at him. There was a comic in Toronto for a while in the mid-'80s who had a prop act, somewhat like the venerable Carrot Top. Since he wasn't going anywhere, he came up with a wrestling persona for himself. He wore an electric-blue outfit, complete with full face mask, and billed himself as Crusher Comic. He quickly developed a small but deeply disturbed following, although he did the same prop act. All he added to it were some wrestling style references, and a raucous, here-comes-the-bad-guy-wrestler opening. He would get the audience into such a frenzy that, usually with 10 or 15 minutes, he would lose control of them completely, which was an amazing thing to watch. Brian's set in Fort McMurray was like that. All of his smart, hip Toronto material went right in the toilet and within fifteen minutes he was screaming "SHUT UP!!" to an angry mob. Finally, he introduced Dawn, who had played a few more bars than Brian had. She did damn well with what she was handed that night. She had a mad, drunken heckler who chased her all over the room, but she was intelligent enough to take the microphone with her, so while she was hiding from this idiot, she could insult him from cover. It was a really impressive performance. By the end, she had the crowd with her and was getting strong response. I went up and I don't remember a thing about my performance, other than I got through it and we got our cash and left.

I topped off the tank at a gas station on the outskirts of town, and we blazed away, money in hand. It was a little after eleven when we left. About an hour outside Fort McMurray, there was an open gas station, but I had just topped the tank of, so I didn't bother stopping there. Which turned out to be a grave error. That was the last open station we found that night. We cruised into Athabasca at around 2:30

in the morning, running dangerously low on fuel. I felt sure there'd be an open station in Athabasca. Of course there would be. There wasn't. I drove twice around that damn town merely to confirm this fact. The Thunderbird had a gas gauge with lights on it. When the tank was full, there were a lot of lights,. As it emptied, the lights went out, one by one. We headed down the highway toward Edmonton.

At this point, I was furious with myself. Here I was, trying like hell to impress this woman and I was running out of gas on a road trip like a goddamned amateur. A road trip in late October in northern Alberta, no less. It was really cold, and the prospect of finding gas was remote at best. With one measly light remaining on the gauge, I saw a sign that said *Rochester-3*. We turned off the highway and made for it.

Rochester was a one-street town. There was a gas station/general store, a grain silo, a bar, and a flophouse. I don't recall a traffic light. We pulled up in front of the gas station and I got out. There was a house next to the station and I was sure the owner lived there. I considered what might happen if I knocked on his door and asked him to reopen for a few minutes. It was 3 a.m. now and he might have a gun, visitors in this area at this hour being rather unusual. I decided it was too risky. The flophouse seemed a better bet. The door was open and we went in. There were a series of doors in the circular lobby, but they were all locked and there was no one about. So we went upstairs, where we found the rooms and a small sitting area with a couple of chairs and ashtrays. Dawn sat down and said, "Why don't we hang out here until the gas station opens?" But I wasn't satisfied. Still seething at my stupidity which got us here, I began trying doors to rooms. After a couple of quiet attempts, one opened. We all went over to have a look. It was a small room, with two beds, one a double, both unmade. The room appeared to have been very recently occupied, but that didn't stop me. We went in. Brian was behind me and I remember thinking that if I went for the double bed, he'd naturally take the single, not wanting to sleep with me. That's what happened, so I at last got to sleep with Dawn, in a shitty little flophouse room in Rochester Alberta. With all our clothes on, including our coats, because the room was very cold. There wasn't much sleep for any of us, with the pipes banging outside the window, and the fear that the occupant might show up at any time. But I did sleep with her. For the first time. It had taken a bad run of luck, but it had finally happened.

She shook me awake at seven, and I said I would go down and gas up the car and they should meet me there. I slipped out of the place without being seen, and, amazingly, so did Dawn and Brian. We gassed up, bought some crappy food with bad coffee, and got the hell and gone out of Rochester. No one, other than the woman at the gas station had seen us. We were phantoms.

After that, Dawn and I were together. I'm not sure what happened on the road that night, but we were boyfriend and girlfriend from that day forward. She says it's because, having made an egregious road error, the first and only time it ever happened to me, I suddenly wasn't so angry. I was humbled by my mistake and she liked that. When we parted a few days later at the airport, we both knew that something special had happened to us. I had the plan all set in my mind. I would move to Los Angeles, marry Dawn, and get my green card. She went back to L.A. and I returned to Toronto, where I broke up with my much younger girlfriend.

I phoned Dawn every day for two straight months. I phoned her in Los Angeles, Honolulu, Oregon, Montana, wherever she was. Every day. In November, I did a gig in St. Louis, Missouri, and I decided to do the trip home in one go after the show Saturday. It would take 14 hours and break my record. (I was into records in those days). I had a small tape recorder and I recorded my thoughts and impressions on it every hour of the drive. Talking to Dawn, telling her where I was, how the trip was going, etc. The first few entries were bright and cheery, or as bright and cheery as could be, but as the drive progressed, I got more and more slurred and incoherent. When I finally made it back to my place in Toronto I sang her a song. John Prine's 'Sleepy-Eyed Boy'. My voice was hard gravel by then. I mailed her the tape. In December, she did a Yoder run in Michigan, and I arranged to meet her in Detroit, and took her to Sarnia to meet my family. Someone took a photo of her sitting on the piano bench in our living room, and when the pictures were developed, my sister asked my mother if she wanted that one in the family album.

"Certainly not," mother sniffed. "She's just another one of John's babes." Mother's perspicacity in these matters was legend, but, on this one occasion, she was wrong.

I went to Los Angeles in January to visit her, and she came to Toronto in February to visit me. We had another western tour scheduled in March of 1988. I gave up my apartment, gave away most of my stuff, and drove to Winnipeg to meet her. We travelled across the prairies into British Columbia, where we crossed the border and I moved to Los Angeles. Fifteen years later, we're still keeping house. One of the reasons we're together, I think, is because we spent much of the early part of our relationship in a car, driving thousands of miles. We crisscrossed the continent four times in those early years, and had adventures along every road.

The one I remember best was a gig we did in Fort Nelson, B.C. It was the start of the trip. We flew to Edmonton and picked up a rental car, a Hyundai Pony. The booker had warned us that the first gig was a long drive, so I figured six hours, eight at the most. That's a long drive, right? But Fort Nelson, at the very top of B.C., was a 12-hour drive, much of it along the famed Alaska highway, which was unfinished then. Parts of it were little more than gravel. There weren't a whole passel of signs, either, so it was four o'clock in the afternoon before we realized just how damn far this gig was. We also knew we were going to be late.

"So what?" Dawn said. "We're the show, right? They can't start until we get there, therefore we can't be late." So on we drove. At one point, we were coming over a little rise, and I saw a Jeep Cherokee parked on our side of the road, with the driver standing there, holding on to the open car door. Just as we pulled abreast of him, a huge black dog came bounding out of the bushes onto the road in front of us. For a second I thought the man had stopped to let his dog take a leak, until I looked more closely and saw that it wasn't a dog. It was a black bear. I got a firsthand look at how fast they are, because he stayed with the Pony for a few seconds, until I floored it to 50 and left him in the dust. I still wonder what the hell the guy was doing outside his car. A few miles later, we were coming around a big bend in the road and up ahead I saw a mother moose and her calf crossing the highway very slowly. I slowed down to avoid hitting them, knowing that if I spooked the mother we were dead meat. I'd seen what a moose can do to a car when she puts her mind to it. We managed to escape that little problem, even getting a photo of mother and child.

We finally pulled into Fort Nelson around nine p.m. The show was scheduled for 8:30 and the room was full. I hurried up to the hotel room to wash my hair while Dawn threw on a show outfit and started the proceedings. She did her 30 solid minutes and introduced me. Everything went fine for the first half-hour of my show, despite the fact that I was a bit punchy after 12 hours behind the wheel. The audience was receptive and appreciative. They probably didn't get a lot of entertainment this far north. The hotel clerk told us that they were supposed to have strippers from Red Deer the week before, but they had called and canceled. That's how far away this gig was. Even strippers wouldn't do it. I went into my musical set grateful that I had only 25 minutes left to go.

But something was wrong. I got to the second dog joke, and I could not recall how it went. Which was paralyzing. First of all, I could do the dog bit stoned, I could do it in an oxygen tent, I could do it under general anaesthesia. I had *never* dried in front of a comedy audience before. Secondly, by then, Dawn never watched the musical set. My stand-up set always had new things in it, but the last 25 minutes were set in stone. They never changed. So Dawn never stayed around for that. But, for some reason, on that night, she did. I was standing there wondering what the hell I was going to say when Dawn's voice clearly called out, "Call him." The key words were all I needed, and I got through that joke. But I was so freaked out by drying up that I now couldn't recall any of the damn dog jokes. Dawn had to call out the key words for every single one. Thank God.

That's why I'm so lucky to be married to a comedienne. At first, one of the really attractive things about this job is that you can't share it with anyone who doesn't do it. It is yours and yours alone. Even actresses don't have any idea what stand-up is like. Then, as the time passes, you come to want to share it with someone. And I could share it with Dawn. She knew all the ups and downs, all the temptations and isolations. She knew she'd better hang around that night in Fort Nelson, tired as she was. She knew I might not be right after 12 hours of driving. She knew.

I started watching the Tonight Show around 1971. I saw most of Steve Martin's sets in the '70s and '80s. I saw Jerry Seinfeld, Ronnie Shakes, Franklin Ajaye, Billy Braver, Dick Shawn, George Carlin, and a host of others. It had been embarrassing as hell to admit to the Globe & Mail reporter in 1983 that Carson was the goal. THE goal. I'd love to have a sitcom, or get acting jobs, or writing jobs, but I'm a comedian first and last. I didn't get into this so I could get famous and stop doing it. That was never the idea.

THE TONIGHT SHOW: 1988/90

Other than Carl Reiner's *The Comic,* with Dick Van Dyke as the self-destructive funnyman, the movies never got it right. In 1981, there was a Canadian movie called *Comics.* Mark Breslin was in it. So were Mike MacDonald, Tony Molesworth, Howard Busgang, Ron Vaudry, and a few others. An actor named Miles Chapin played the young, hopeful comedian who gets his hopes dashed on the unforgiving rock of showbiz. The only really funny line Miles had was unintentional. He'd been fired from the sitcom he was supposed to star in, and he's in the car with his girlfriend. With the silliest look on his face, he says, "This sure is an ugly business." I laughed my head off.

Mike and Howard were the best things in the picture. Especially Mike, who played a comedian who goes crazy and winds up in an asylum. There were also a couple of mildly funny scenes of a group of comedians, led by Peter Aykroyd, going around playing practical jokes on people and businesses. But of course in real life this never happens. Comedians stay home, sleep late, smoke dope, watch TV, and try to think of funny things.

Then there was the Tom Hanks-Sally Field movie, called *Punchline.* It had, to its credit, *one* absolutely truthful moment. Late in the movie there's a competition at the comedy club, the winner to get some sort of network deal (yeah right). All the comedians are awaiting the judges' decision in the basement locker room (I've never been in a comedy club that has a locker room). Everyone expects Tom Hanks to win. He obviously did the best set. But no, the owner says, as a matter of fact, Tom did not win. Sally Field is disgusted by this, and says, "If Tom didn't win, then it's a farce. Take my name out. I'm out." Another comedian joins in, "Yeah, I'm out, too."

Still another, "I'm out." Then, a comic played by Taylor Negron says, "Uh, I'm still in, OK?" That was the best moment, and the most real thing about this job I ever saw in a movie.

Here's what really happened. I got to Los Angeles in the spring of 1988. My manager was Ed Adler, a young Turk in the management company Moress, Nanas, Golden. Herb Nanas managed Albert Brooks and the late Bill Hicks, among others. He had real pull in those days. He got me a prime spot at the Improv within a week of my arrival. Budd Friedman, the owner, and Jim McCawley, the Tonight Show booker, would be there to see me. I'd been on the road for almost three years without a break, so I was as hot as I could be. I went on, did 'Comedy's Better', and just murdered. Budd Friedman later said that I restored his faith in stand-up comedy that night, a fact no amount of modesty will let me leave out of this story. Jim McCawley loved me as well. Herb Nanas was beside himself as he sat with me afterward. He couldn't stop talking.

"You're gonna do the Tonight Show. You're gonna do all the shows. You're gonna get a network deal. You're gonna have your own sitcom. You're gonna have a big house in Malibu..." And on and on and on. I may have even been swept up by his enthusiasm and believed a word of it.

Soon after that first triumph, the tweaking began. McCawley wasn't satisfied with the set. He felt that 'Comedy's Better' was a bit too sexual in tone, and we should water it down. He didn't want Johnny to be offended. As well, I started doing fewer and fewer shows. In 1987 I did 312 shows, an average of six a week, almost all of them full length, an hour or more. In L.A. I was maybe managing two 10- to 15-minute sets a week. So I came in hot, but I didn't stay hot. My act was also constructed in such a way that if you started taking jokes out, there was a danger of the whole thing falling apart. And it did.

By August, when McCawley saw me for the fifth or sixth time, the set was just hideous. Just bad from beginning to end. I'd really lost my edge and my confidence. He told me to write a new six-minute set, and to call him when it was ready. The new six minutes took a year to write. No joke. It had taken me three or four years to make 'Comedy's Better' perfect, so a single year for a new set isn't really that long. I needed a new opening to my show, and it was a year before I had a set I thought McCawley would like. I started, as I urge most amateurs to start, with my name. *My name is John Wing, and Wing is a Chinese name. In Chinese, it means the arm of a bird.* With that joke, I started the second phase of my career.

There were other factors at play. I didn't know it would take a year to write another set, so I was still gung-ho to do the show, hoping I would do the show, waiting for the call, dreaming about it *all the time*. I was selfish about it, too. I wanted to be the first guy from my group at Yuk Yuks to do it. I was searingly competitive about that. I had Mike MacDonald, whom I considered the most serious threat, Jeremy

WORKING UP TO "TONIGHT": I was doing a lot of other shows. Evening At The Improv, Improv Tonite, Comic Strip Live, MTV's Half-Hour Comedy Hour, Caroline's Comedy Hour, you name it. One of them aired in June of 1990, and Jay Leno happened to see it.

Hotz not far behind, Steve Fromstein and Jeff Rothpan rounding the clubhouse turn. After Dawn and I got married in the summer of 1989, and just before I finally showed McCawley my new set, we went to Toronto for a working honeymoon. In the green room of the downtown club, I encountered Mike one night, and instead of telling me how much money he was making, which was what he usually did, he told me he had the Tonight Show. *Had* it. Just a formality of giving him a firm date. He was on the list, no word of a lie. He was positively gleeful about it. Or as gleeful as Mike can get. With Dawn back at the hotel, I almost cried. I was like a child. *He doesn't get to do it, I GET TO DO IT! He's got all the gigs, all the money, all the deals. This is MINE!* It was all Dawn could do to console me.

I showed the new set to McCawley when we returned to Los Angeles. But it wasn't good enough. It wasn't consistent enough, he said. He was right. Some nights it did very well. Other nights they stared at me like I was being hanged. I fiddled and fiddled with it. Showed it to him in October. No soap. In December. Sorry, pal. Twice in March, because the first time it killed. The second time it bombed. Back to the board. I recall thinking about what Herb Nanas said that night in April of 1988 when April of 1990 passed and I still hadn't done it. Of course, by then I wasn't represented by Herb anymore.

Mike had not done the show. He was probably trying to intimidate me. He was no doubt just realizing then, after knowing me nine years, that I was a real rival and might easily pass him on this curve. Our rivalry stayed rather intense for a while, but it was something we never spoke of to each other. A few years later, I did Late Night With Ralph

Benmergui in Toronto a week before Mike did it. I had a good set, with six applause breaks. The next week I was playing Yuk Yuks in London, Ontario, and I happened to see Mike's set in the green room between shows. It was the early winter of 1994, because Mike opened by saying, *Great to be here. I haven't been back to Toronto since the Blue Jays won the world series.* Which got a tremendous ovation, naturally. Mike looked right into the camera, and in his clipped, smug little voice, he said, "That's *one.*" I knew he was talking to me. I confirmed it later with Mike. Joel Axler, one of the show's producers, had been harping on my set the whole afternoon before the taping. "Wing got six applause breaks , Mike. How many are you gonna get, huh? How many, huh? You gonna get as many as Wing did? Are you?" That's the really special thing about our business; that it's populated with such an abnormally classy group of people.

In the meantime I was doing a lot of other shows. Evening At The Improv, Improv Tonite, Comic Strip Live, MTV's Half-Hour Comedy Hour, Caroline's Comedy Hour, you name it. One of them aired in June of 1990, and Jay Leno happened to see it. I had a joke in the set he really liked. *Last night my parents had a huge argument about abortion. But Mom was right, it is spelled t-i-o-n.* A week or so later, I was at the Improv and, spotting me, Jay called me over to his table. He was quite complimentary, and said I should do the Tonight Show with him as guest host. I told him to talk to McCawley, and he did. In August, McCawley saw the set do well at the Improv and finally I got my date. September 18th, 1990. Since I would be with Jay and not Johnny, the pressure wouldn't be so great on Jim McCawley. If I ate it, he could always blame it on Jay.

"*He* wanted him. I didn't think he was ready, but Jay wanted the guy on..." I started opening all my shows with *the* set. I would do a set anywhere that September. I practiced the piece at least 10 times in the last two weeks. It still wasn't consistent, though. One night it'd be great and the next night down in flames. I couldn't figure out what it was missing, and it was so easy, I should have known, but I was too paranoid, too close to it.

I don't think I told too many people about the date. No, wait a minute. That's not me. I probably told everyone including the guy who bused my table at Denny's. My name was in the TV Guide again. Not to put down Joan Rivers, or even Arsenio Hall, but this was the big one. The biggest show in North America for a comedian. I had studied 10 years for a six-minute exam, with *my whole career* riding on the outcome. And I am not exaggerating. I didn't sleep a lot the last two or three days, but September 18th finally arrived. Dawn and I drove to NBC studios in Burbank that afternoon. I had typed out the set, word for word, and had it folded in my jacket pocket. For many days, it had never left my person.

Nervous doesn't truly describe how I was feeling. Jay came by the dressing room (another fruit basket and bottle of wine) and was very encouraging. He said, "The boss is away, let's have some fun." He really helped me calm down a bit. I went into the green room with Dawn to watch the first half of the show. Tom Snyder, who was doing a radio show in the building somewhere, kept coming in and stealing food from the snack table. Ed Begley, Jr. was the guest before me. McCawley came and collected me and we stood behind the curtain. *The* curtain. The curtain of the Tonight Show, in the studio NBC built for Bob Hope in the fifties. Jim would hold open the curtain for me, and his hand was on it, ready to go. I tried to take deep breaths. Suddenly, he looked at me and smiled.

"Don't forget your jokes," he said. I froze at the thought, then whipped out my set sheet and frantically scanned down the page. Jay went into my intro. Then my name was called. On the tape, if you look closely, you can see me stuffing the set sheet back into my breast pocket as I come out. I was wearing my navy-blue double breasted suit. The suit I got married in. *Walk slow.* Mark Breslin's advice came back to me. Slowly I strolled to the spot, a piece of yellow tape on the studio floor. My heart was beating like it had never beaten before. Like a trip-hammer. I look really calm on the tape, but inside my chest it was *Bongo Bongo Bongo I Don't Want To Leave The Congo.* My last conscious thought was, "Man, if I have a heart attack right here, it will be really embarrassing." Then I opened my mouth and gave them the first joke. After that, I don't really have any recollection. I've seen it on tape a few hundred times, so I know what happened, but I performed the set in a zombified state. An intense, heightened automatic pilot. Virtually everything I said killed. I got 11 applause breaks in six minutes. It was just like my first set 10 years before. I locked into rhythm and rode it to the end, and everything I did got laughs. It was better than sex. And, nowadays, a lot longer, too.

The set never bombed again anywhere. It always killed. Because I knew it was funny after that night. I never had any more doubt about it. What had been missing was my attitude. Should have known. Always lessons to re-learn, jokes to re-work. What do I want to be talking about next week? Next month? Next year? Stay tuned, we'll be right back.

There were nights, utterly common in every way, when I was doing the old stuff, the 'greatest hits', and my mind would wander so far away that duplicity of what I was doing and where my brain was would amaze me. It was similar to a long boring night drive, where for miles upon miles, I would steer the car unthinkingly, without actually taking note of anything I was doing, my mind focused on some imaginary conversation with me playing all the parts, or some joke I was searching for. Then I'd 'wake up', and realize that I'd driven a hundred damn miles without paying attention. In my 20s, it sometimes made me laugh. Eventually it became frightening.

TRAVEL DAY: 1988

THE SHOW IS over. Star Search International. It was Lee Evans from England, Tamayo Otsuki from Japan, and me from Canada. A one-off. Five thousand to the winner. Lee won. The judges liked his physical impression of a basketball losing all its air and then being pumped full again. Wish I'd thought of that. I'm standing in the parking lot with Ed Adler, my manager. He gives me a joint for the road. It's ten-thirty p.m. I have to get going.

It's a Saturday night in late November, 1988. I'm due in Calgary. Dawn has already flown there. I have a show there in less than 48 hours. I also have a car with a Canadian license plate, leased in Toronto and insured for Canada. I've been driving it in California now for seven months. It's time to get it back home. I say goodbye to Ed.

I stop off at a friend's house and he gives me two more joints. Three might do it, if I'm careful. It's 11 now. I hit the 101 eastbound to Interstate 10 eastbound. Just outside Montclair, California, I pick up Interstate 15, also going east. This road goes, amazingly, all the way to Calgary. The car is running well and I'm feeling good. A bottle of coke in the cupholder and some sad Irish tunes on the tape deck.

I go over the San Bernardino mountains, glad that it's so dark that I can't see any of the dropoffs. They climb past 5,000 feet and are roller coasters of pushing the car up a steep grade, and braking hard as it tears down the other side. After what seems like hours, I get over the last hill onto a flatter road. I stop for gas in Baker, California, thinking of the old Tom Waits song. *Pullin' into Baker on a New Year's Eve. One eye on the pistol and the other on the door. One eye on the pistol and the other on the door.* I've never driven this route; never been to any of the cities along the way except Calgary. It's after two a.m. now, and I'm a little tired, so I smoke a third of one of the joints. That's better.

After a while, I start thinking that I must be getting close to the Nevada border. Surely there'll be a sign. Then, in the distance I see two enormous casinos on either side of the highway. The names, so brightly lit you can read them from a few miles away, say WHISKEY PETE'S and KACTUS KATE'S. Still no sign. Finally, less than half a mile from the casino exit, a small sign announces *Welcome To Nevada – The Silver State.*

Twenty minutes later I notice the sky ahead of me is lit up in a rosy rainbow of colour. Odd for a night drive. It can't be the northern lights. Then, over the hill, I see in the distance a city like no other. Las Vegas. The lights are truly unbelievable. As I pass through and leave it behind, I note in the rear view that the sky lights stay visible for more than an hour. I don't turn and look back, for fear of turning into a pillar of salt. Outside of Vegas, the sign said, *Salt Lake City – 523 Mi.* Jesus.

I pass Mesquite, Nevada around 4:30 a.m. and then slide through a 20-odd mile stretch of northern Arizona. I can now say I've been to Arizona. I smoke another third of a joint and my fourteenth cigarette and as dawn breaks, eight hours into the drive, I hit the Utah border.

I spend the whole day driving across Utah, as the road weaves and bends through the magnificent Rocky Mountains. Each curve brings forth breathtaking sights. Sights I have never seen. Snow-capped peaks everywhere, rising out of the earth in their own crazed pattern. I begin to long for the flatlands of southern Ontario. The driving is easier there because there's nothing to look at. Utah is gorgeous, and like Nebraska, it's a long way across. I'm yawning again as I reach Salt Lake City, 13 hours into the drive. It's a little after noon, or one p.m., depending on what time zone you have entered or just left.

The day flies by. As I cross the border into Idaho, I've broken my all-time single sitting driving record. I'm at 15 straight hours. Over 900 miles. I see a sign that says *Idaho Falls — 275 miles.* If I push it, I can be there in four hours. I push it.

The sun is just down as I pull into a Holiday Inn on the outskirts of Idaho Falls, Idaho at six p.m. Nineteen hours behind the wheel. Twelve hundred miles behind me. I am asleep within 10 minutes of entering my room.

I awake with a start. The clock says midnight. I've slept six hours. I could go....two more? Maybe? I look outside. A blizzard. Time to go. I get up, splash on some water and clothing, leave the key and hump it back to I-15. Along the edge of Wyoming and into Montana in the dead of night. I finish the second joint and am now wide awake. At Butte, the road splits and I head for Helena and Great Falls. At dawn, I pull into Sweetgrass on the border and buy a quick breakfast. Then across the border into Alberta. Past Lethbridge, losing my sight every few minutes in the bright sun, I finally limp into Calgary and find my way to the hotel. It's 11:30 a.m. mountain time. I am exhausted and elated. Almost 2,000 miles in 35 and a half hours with a six- hour sleep stop.

Dawn is angry with me. I didn't call from L.A. or anywhere else on the road to let her know I was okay. That was insensitive of me. "I'm okay," I say. It doesn't help. The fact that I made it safely doesn't mitigate the circumstances at all. I wonder how long she'll be mad. Probably not long. *(Must nap now. Show in eight hours.)*

ACKNOWLEDGMENTS

FIRST THINGS FIRST. My friend, Marty Gervais, is the reason this book was written. He bugged me to do it. He pushed me to do it, and he assured that I would do it by giving me what I need most when writing. A ridiculous deadline.

My beautiful, long-suffering wife, Dawn Greene, read the manuscript first and made several excellent suggestions, which I resented.

Thanks to my brother, Richard A.V. Wing, whose memory for jokes I have long forgotten is only one of his great abilities. Thanks to Wayne Flemming, Tim Molloy, and Juri Strenge, who sat with me and gave me their impressions of the time I was trying to remember and recreate. Thanks to Michel Demers, production manager of the Rhapsody of the Seas, who gave me his workstation where the bulk of this book was composed. Thanks to Katherine Quinsey and everyone at the English Department of the University of Windsor, who encouraged me and let me teach creative writing, the only thing on earth I like doing better than stand-up comedy. Thanks to Howard, Andrew, Chris, Jackie, and Wendy at Lapides Entertainment. Thanks to the Canada Council.

Special thanks to John Ditsky, who had more to do with me being a writer than anyone else.

Marquis Book Printing Inc.

Québec, Canada
2008

Printed in Canada